QTS

English for Secondary Teachers

An Audit and Self-Study Guide

Alison Johnson

Secondary English Advisor
Colin Harrison

Letts

EDUCATIONAL

Aldine Place
London
W12 8AW

Tel: 0181-740 2268
Fax: 0181-743 8451
e-mail: he@lettsed.co.uk

Acknowledgements

The publishers and author would like to thank Colin Harrison for his constructive comment on these materials. Special thanks also to Roger Trend of the School of Education, University of Exeter, for providing continuing guidance and co-ordination of the series.

A CIP catalogue record is available from the British Library

ISBN 1-85805-353-6
Copyright Alison Johnson © 1998

Designed and edited by Topics – The Creative Partnership, Exeter

Printed and bound in Great Britain by Progressive Printing (UK) Ltd, Leigh-on-Sea, Essex

Contents

About the series

The Letts QTS Series offers support for all those preparing to become teachers and working towards Qualified Teacher Status (QTS). The content, teaching approaches and practical ideas are useful for trainee teachers, teacher tutors and mentors, and teacher educators in higher education.

The Letts QTS Series addresses the new standards for QTS and the content of the Initial Teacher Training National Curriculum (ITTNC). These are central to the improvement of standards in schools. The series is specifically designed to help all trainee teachers cover the content of the ITTNC and achieve the national standards in order to be awarded QTS.

The short series handbook *QTS: A Practical Introduction* gives trainees an overview of the QTS requirement and a more detailed interpretation of each standard.

The other books in the Letts QTS Series offer trainees the chance to audit their knowledge of the content of the subjects in the ITTNC, pinpoint areas of further work, and use support materials to develop their knowledge.

There are two Letts QTS Series books for each subject:

Book 1 addresses trainees' subject knowledge at their own level by offering a systematic and comprehensive guide to the subject knowledge requirements of the ITTNC. Trainees can check their own knowledge of the subject against that specified in the ITTNC. Section one provides a comprehensive **audit** of this subject knowledge and understanding, with helpful **feedback** and follow-up set out in section two. Having identified areas of subject knowledge for attention, trainees can then use the support materials in section three to develop

key ideas and map out their **personal learning plan**.

Book 2 for each subject is a handbook of **lesson plans**, **knowledge** and **methods**. This provides details of carefully selected lessons which illustrate effective teaching. It shows how lesson planning and classroom teaching draw on a high level of subject knowledge. It demonstrates how carefully integrated whole-class teaching and group and individual work can be designed to ensure that pupils make progress in their learning.

The Letts QTS Series aims to break down the requirements of QTS into manageable units so that trainees can evaluate and improve their knowledge of each subject. The books in the series are written in a straightforward way by authors who are all experienced teachers, teacher educators, researchers, writers and specialists in their subject areas.

About this book

This book is designed for all prospective teachers of English in secondary schools. Whatever your background, there will be some areas of English subject knowledge that are less familiar to you than others. These may be in the domains of literary, linguistic or literacy studies. This book helps you identify areas of strength and weakness for yourself. It then develops areas of weakness through careful explanation of tasks and suggests ways of developing all areas further. There are three chapters:

- **Auditing your knowledge**
- **Feedback**
- **Developing your knowledge**

The **audit** contains a number of tasks in sections that relate to the subject knowledge set out in Section C of the ITTNC (Initial Teacher Training National Curriculum). The **feedback** gives you three kinds of response to the **audit**: answers, explanation and development, and advice for further action. The chapter on **developing your knowledge** is a short one that points you in the direction of further study; detailed coverage is obviously impossible in a book of this length.

The scope of knowledge required to teach English at secondary level is particularly

wide because it covers vast areas, not only of literary and linguistic studies, but also of the development of literacy. Literacy is itself diverse, covering knowledge and skills of reading, writing, speaking and listening, and computer literacy. This knowledge, although principally the responsibility of English, serves all areas of the curriculum.

It is difficult to separate pedagogical knowledge from subject knowledge, because the latter is essential for the former. In other words, in order to teach one needs both subject knowledge and knowledge about teaching and learning. Pedagogical knowledge will be presented in a second book, but ideas will also be gained in the feedback to the tasks contained in this book and in notes given in the right-hand column of each page.

At first glance, the **audit** may seem rather daunting. Do not feel that you need to tackle it all at one sitting. You may find it easier to start with sections and tasks in areas where you have greater confidence and read the feedback to these before returning to more challenging tasks. Some of the tasks may involve you in some research, reading or self-study. The audit is not a test, so do not feel that having to look for an answer is cheating. Far from it. Any work that you do in response to a task, which develops your knowledge and

understanding of English, will be beneficial. You are not auditing your knowledge merely to check it off as something to consign to memory; it will be knowledge that becomes an integral part of your development as a teacher and a resource for teaching.

The **feedback** chapter suggests self-study tasks for developing your knowledge. Keep a written record of any study you do in response, as you may be asked to show how you have developed weaker areas and demonstrate evidence of areas of particular strength. You can use this record to target particular knowledge areas for development. In addition, if you carry out any subsequent audits, record your progress and development and target any remaining weaknesses.

A **glossary** of key literary and linguistic terms is provided at the back of the book. This is merely a sample, and terms are very briefly defined, but the definitions will serve as a starting point, quick reference, or aide-memoire. Also at the back of the book is a **further reading** section containing all the books referred to elsewhere.

The **personal learning plan** suggests ways of recording initial levels of knowledge, action and further progress. A template for this record is provided.

Auditing your knowledge

What is English subject knowledge and why audit?

English subject knowledge covers areas of literary study, linguistics and literacy, and knowledge of the National Curriculum for English and the syllabuses for GCSE and A level.

You may believe that you can read and teach novels without complex knowledge of syntax or stylistics or that detailed knowledge of the phonological system is unnecessary. The answer to the question *Why audit?* must therefore be that knowledge is a powerful resource that can enhance the appreciation, interpretation and meaning of text and enable you to be articulate in your explanations and teaching. Knowledge is therefore a tool, rather than an attribute to be collected.

The purpose of the audit

This may be your first attempt at auditing your knowledge in English; alternatively you may have audited your knowledge already (in which case you can use this audit to check and record your progress). Whatever the case, you should understand that there will be a great variety of breadth of subject knowledge, depending on your background in English. GCSE, A level and undergraduate degree courses may have been broadly literature or language based, or may have provided a balance in both areas. As a result, you will find some of the knowledge very familiar and some almost entirely new. This is the purpose of the audit: to identify areas of strength and weakness for yourself. Early identification will allow you to target weaknesses and build on strengths. Subsequent uses of the audit will allow you to measure your progress towards a sound knowledge of English.

This is not a test, but you may wish to mark your answers. The audit has been written in a way that allows you to do this. Almost all of the tasks have questions with clearly definable answers. This is not intended to give the impression that English is ultimately quantifiable, but to allow direct answers that enable you to assess your level of knowledge.

The content of the audit

Each section contains tasks covering a particular area of the knowledge outlined in the ITTNC for English. Section A, for example, contains a task related to the technical terminology of English. The knowledge contained in this section does not have to be audited but is knowledge which you 'must know and understand' (ITTNC paragraph 27a). It has therefore been included here.

Sections B to G cover the knowledge specified in paragraph 28 of the ITTNC and are appropriate for the range of 11–19 courses and for students on Key Stage 2/3 courses, although in the latter case you should in addition be able to demonstrate knowledge related to the Key Stage 2 programmes of study. For example, in Section A, knowledge of basic terms such as *author, plot* and *setting* should be known and, in Section G, knowledge of a range of texts must include children's literature including modern and long-established children's fiction, modern and classic poetry, texts from a variety of cultures and traditions, and myths, legends and traditional stories. For help with this, consult another Letts publication, *English for Primary Teachers: An Audit and Self-Study Guide*, written by David Wray and Jane Medwell (1997).

The knowledge specified in paragraph 29 of the ITTNC is not explicitly audited here, although many of the tasks cover this knowledge. The breadth and depth of knowledge required for post-16 study in language and literature is probably best audited through a sustained piece of writing for a written assignment.

Extracts of text are used throughout. All been specifically written or selected because they exemplify the features being audited in a particular section.

How to approach the audit

You will need to spend about six hours completing the audit. For this reason, it is suggested that you allot three periods of two hours, dividing the audit into three: Sections A and B; Sections C and D and Sections E to G. Record your answers on paper for marking and future reference. Some answers will involve you in copying out sentences from the audit if you want to avoid annotating the text in the book to allow for future use. You may wish to carry out one part of the audit, mark it and read the feedback before moving on to the next section of audit tasks.

Tasks give examples of answers to enable you to make your best attempt and in order to remove any ambiguity in the question. Attempt every question, even if you identify it as one that is auditing knowledge which appears completely new to you, and remember that the breadth of your subject knowledge is dependent on your background in English. Difficulty in some areas is to be expected. If a particular section seems to be taking a long time to complete, summarize your thoughts and note that you need to spend time reading the feedback to this section in detail.

On the first occasion you will be assessing your initial level of knowledge. You might wish to repeat the audit midway through or towards the end of your course in order to identify progress and any further study required. Record your answers to any further audit of knowledge to assess progress.

Ways of following up the audit are suggested in the feedback and development chapters. Remember that the purpose of the audit is not to test what you don't know; it is intended to help you identify secure knowledge and gaps in that knowledge.

Section A:

Technical terms in English language and literature

Task A – Technical terms

A sample of technical terms from the metalanguage of English language and literature is shown below. Following these are explanations, definitions or examples that illustrate them. Match each term to the most appropriate definition by linking each letter to a number.

Tips, clues and advice are given in this column throughout the *Audit*. Use these to help you if you get stuck.

Metalanguage

e.g.   *metalanguage* – Literally means 'about language'.
    The answer is: 11(b).

1. *adverb*
2. *anaphoric reference*
3. *allusion*
4. *bound morpheme*
5. *cloze procedure*
6. *double negative*
7. *ellipsis*
8. *grapheme*
9. *homonym*
10. *implied reader*
11. *metalanguage*
12. *modal auxiliary*
13. *pathetic fallacy*
14. *post-structuralism*
15. *register*
16. *schwa*
17. *semiotics*
18. *syntax*
19. *verb – intransitive*
20. *verb – transitive*

Many of the following audit tasks ask for definitions and explanations of terminology, further developing this area.

(a) *Stopped* in the sentence: *The train stopped.*

(b) Literally means 'about language'.

(c) *Stopped* in the sentence: *The policeman stopped the traffic.*

(d) A letter of the alphabet.

(e) The unstressed vowel sound in spoken words such as: *independent.*

(f) The way we choose to speak or write, based on formality, choice of vocabulary, and purpose of text.

(g) E.g. the word *plot,* which is polysemantic, although meaning can usually be found in context: *The plot was hatched. Plot the co-ordinates on a graph. The novel's plot was complex.*

(h) E.g. *I didn't have no dinner.* A feature of non-standard English.

(i) Demonstrated in the second of the two following clauses linked by but:
    | *I love hamburgers* | *but* | *hate onions.* | (Clauses are indicated by: | .)

(j) Is concerned with sentences, clauses, phrases and their structure, including knowledge of word classes.

(k) E.g. *gently, now.*

(l) E.g. *can, may, should.*

(m) Giving human emotions to nature as in 'autumn suns / Smiling at eve upon the quiet sheaves' (Keats).

(n) A reference, often to myth or historical event, which may be direct or indirect and creates complexity of meaning.

(o) Where readers fill in missing words in a text by using syntactic and contextual knowledge, giving indications of reading behaviours.

(p) E.g. *they* in: *Ben and Mike left Wembley early. They had seen enough.*

(q) E.g. *-ful* as in *dreadful.* Carries meaning, but cannot stand alone.

(r) The study of signs or symbols used in film, poetry and novels.

(s) A role described by Wolfgang Iser.

(t) An approach to texts that presupposes no single meaning or reading.

Section B:

The lexical system of spoken and written language

Morpheme

Affix

Prefix, suffix and base

Inflection and derivation

Task B1 – Morphology and semantics

The structure of English words can be analysed as units of meaning, or morphemes. Some words consist of one unit of meaning (one morpheme); others consist of a number of units. These units are affix (prefix and suffix) and base (also called root or stem). Affixes may be inflectional or derivational.

e.g. *dogs* consists of two morphemes: base *dog*; inflectional plural suffix *-s*

circumnavigated consists of four morphemes: derivational prefix *circum-*; base *navig*; derivational suffix *-ate*; inflectional past tense suffix *-(e)d*

Word class

Tense

Each morpheme carries meaning, with the affixes added to the base giving information such as word class or tense.

Look at the list of words below. Segment the words according to the number of morphemes in each. Decide whether the morphemes are bases, or prefixes or suffixes (derivational or inflectional).

(a) *concluded* (d) *hyperactivity* (g) *blackbird*
(b) *boat* (e) *quickest* (h) *untie*
(c) *supermarket* (f) *reverts*

Blackbird differs from the other words here and provides a challenge.

Meaning

Prefixes and suffixes carry particular meanings. Give the common meaning for each of the following affixes and an example of a word containing it.

(i) *con-* (k) *infra-* (m) *-or* (o) *dis-*
(j) *sub-* (l) *inter-* (n) *-oid* (p) *dys-*

Resist the temptation to look up these affixes. Instead, think of a few words with each, and their meanings.

Task B2 – Semantic relations

In well-written texts, a multiplicity of meanings exists between the words that are used. The different relationships of meaning that are created are called semantic relations. These are relationships of synonymy, antonymy or hyponymy. In addition, meaning can be ambiguous because of the polysemantic nature of a word; it may be a homonym.

Synonymy, antonymy and hyponymy

Ambiguity

Homonym

Match (a) to (f) below with the examples given. You will need to locate the words that illustrate each relationship in the sentences.

(a) *synonymy* (c) *hyponymy* (e) *ambiguous meaning*
(b) *antonymy* (d) *co-hyponyms* (f) *homonyms*

1. Shells cascaded from the skies, landing not far from the soldiers as they marched along the shore, shells and pebbles crunching beneath their boots.
2. Mallards, Canada geese and swans swam on the river, heedless of the boaters.
3. Her abode was conveniently situated near her work, but it is at home that we now find our heroine.

Look for the words in each sentence that have a relationship between them and then think about what that relationship is.

9

4. She blew hot and cold; one day she favoured change and the next she opposed it.
5. There was an amazing array of food: salads, fish, freshly baked bread, pickles and dips.
6. Our friend on the back benches is 'green', in several senses of the word.

Task B3 – Semantics and variation

Variation according to user and use

The meaning carried by individual words can vary according to dialect, era, genre, mode, audience, idiolect, collocation or status of the text. Similarly, choice of words is motivated by the use to which they are being put, involving variation of speaker attitude, purpose and position in relation to the listener or reader. The social or generic context and use of words affects their meaning.

(a) Look at the words below. For each word say something about the likely user (speaker or writer) and the expected social or generic context.

gee-gee   *trusty steed*   *equine colic*

Lexical choice
Synonym

(b) The following task aims to make you think about word choice by getting you to consider synonyms of the word *home*, of which there are many – *residence, pad, property* to name but a few. The fact that there are so many possible choices indicates that there is a need for a range of words to suit particular genres, levels of formality, idiomatic phrases and strong collocations.

> There are, in fact, no true synonyms, since very few alternatives are completely interchangeable.

Lexical restriction

Each of the sentences below has a gap that should be filled with a word meaning *home*. You need to consider which word is most appropriate and try to identify the reason for your choice, suggesting any restriction or motivation of meaning or usage. Do not use the word *home* in any of the sentences, but you may consider where it could be placed, as well as sentences in which it would not be appropriate, and the reasons why.

1. An official dinner was held at the Governor's _____ .
2. I call this humble _____ home.
3. When I was younger, I had a bachelor _____ , but now we're in a modern semi.
4. My bruvver's _____ is down Lambeth.
5. Snails are most abundant in a damp, leafy _____ .
6. The _____ is available for immediate occupation.
7. The _____ was uninhabited, being barely more than a shelter from the elements.

> Find synonyms for *home*.

Task B4 – Phonemes and graphemes

Letter to sound correspondence

The alphabet we use consists of 26 letters, made up of consonants and vowels. We use these letters to write around 44 sounds of English. Consequently letters and combinations of letters represent a range of sounds; there is not a one-to-one correspondence between sound and letter.

The grapho-phonic system

A number of technical terms are needed to describe the grapho-phonic system. A list of these terms is given on the following page. Define each term and choose the appropriate example from the eight shown.

e.g.   *grapheme* – A grapheme is one of the 26 letters of the alphabet.

/ɔɪ/ in *v<u>oi</u>ce   <u>n</u>ight   <u>wr</u>ite   w<u>ee</u>p   ca<u>ts</u>   dog<u>s</u>   witt<u>y</u>

/ʌ/ in *c<u>u</u>p*

(a) *unvoiced consonant*   (d) *short vowel phoneme*   (g) *silent consonant*

(b) *vowel grapheme*   (e) *vowel digraph*   (h) *voiced consonant*

(c) *diphthong*   (f) *consonant trigraph*

> Some of the terms describe the graphic system and some describe the phonic system.

Phonemic segmentation

Task B5 – Phonemic and syllabic segmentation

(a) Identify the number of vowel and consonant phonemes in each of the following words. Segment the words into phonemic units.

e.g.   *sauce* has three phonemes: two consonants and one vowel:

/sɔːs/ (s/au/ce)

> Sound the words out and don't be distracted by the number of letters.

(a) *thought*   (c) *elect*   (e) *see*

(b) *enemy*   (d) *washing*   (f) *runner*

Syllabic segmentation
Stressed syllable

(b) Identify the number of syllables in the following words when they are spoken. Segment the words into syllables. Indicate the stressed syllable in each word.

e.g.   *racket* has two syllables: rāck / ĕt

> A syllable is similar to a beat in music.

(g) *elephant*   (i) *notes*   (k) *Worcester*

(h) *unselfish*   (j) *chocolate*   (l) *ridiculous*

Task B6 – Phonology and poetic effect

Poetry uses sound for particular effect. Read the following extract aloud, considering the contribution of phonological features such as rhyme, alliteration and use of homophone. List the features related to phonology and give an example from the poem for each. You may also wish to comment on the semantic effect of a particular feature.

> Read the poem out loud to yourself more than once.

Then she,
Sitting beneath the midmost forest tree,
145 *For pity sang this roundelay:*

'O Sorrow,
Why dost borrow
The natural hue of health, from vermeil lips? –
To give maiden blushes
150 *To the white rose bushes?*
Or is't thy dewy hand the daisy tips?

'O Sorrow
Why dost borrow
The lustrous passion from a falcon-eye? –
155 *To give the glow-worm light?*
Or, on a moonless night,
To tinge, on syren shores, the salt sea-spry?

'O Sorrow,
Why dost borrow
160 The mellow ditties from a mourning tongue? –
To give at evening pale
Unto the nightingale,
That thou mayst listen the cold dews among?

'O Sorrow
165 Why dost borrow
Heart's lightness from the merriment of May? –
A lover would not tread
A cowslip on the head,
Though he should dance from eve till peep of day –
170 Nor any drooping flower
Held sacred for thy bower,
Wherever he may sport himself and play.

'To Sorrow
I bade good-morrow,
175 And thought to leave her far away behind.
But cheerly, cheerly,
She loves me dearly;
She is so constant to me, and so kind:
I would deceive her
180 And so leave her,
But ah! she is so constant and so kind.

(Lines 143–181 from Keats's 'Endymion' book IV.)

Section C:

The grammatical system of spoken and written language

Task C1 – Word class

Word class

When Alice, in *Through the Looking Glass*, comes across the following poem, she says that it is 'rather hard to understand' and 'Somehow it seems to fill my head with ideas – only I don't exactly know what they are! However, *somebody* killed *something*: that's clear, at any rate'.

Grammar

'Jabberwocky' has been used in many books and courses to teach the concept of word class and grammar, so no apologies are made for including it here.

(a) Use your knowledge of English to replace Lewis Carroll's invented words, which are underlined, and give the word class of each word (e.g. noun, verb, adjective) using those 'ideas' that fill your head.

Jabberwocky

'Twas <u>brillig</u>, and the <u>slithy</u> <u>toves</u>
Did <u>gyre</u> and <u>gimble</u> in the <u>wabe</u>;
All <u>mimsy</u> were the <u>borogoves</u>,
And the <u>mome</u> <u>raths</u> <u>outgrabe</u>.

Use the support of word order and common suffixes to help you replace the items.

'Beware the Jabberwock, my son!
The jaws that bite, the claws that catch!
Beware the Jubjub bird, and shun
The _frumious_ Bandersnatch!'

He took his _vorpal_ sword in hand:
Long time the _manxome_ foe he sought –
So rested he by the Tumtum tree,
And stood awhile in thought.

And as in _uffish_ thought he stood,
The Jabberwock, with eyes of flame,
Came _whiffling_ through the _tulgey_ wood,
And _burbled_ as it came!

(b) The words that Lewis Carroll invents are restricted to three or four word classes. The nine most common word classes in English include these. You should now try to identify all nine.

Assign each of the 26 words in stanza three to one of these categories: _noun, adjective, main verb, auxiliary verb, adverb, pronoun, preposition, conjunction, determiner_ (including articles).

He took his vorpal sword in hand:
Long time the manxome foe he sought –
So rested he by the Tumtum tree,
And stood awhile in thought.

You will not find an example of an auxiliary verb in this stanza, but there is one in the longer extract above, and you should try to identify it.

Word function

Task C2 – Word function

Word classes have precise functions within the sentence. For example, prepositions give an indication of place or position of the action or actors in the sentence. They introduce prepositional phrases.

e.g. They danced _in_ the ballroom. She walked _into_ the room.

Describe the function of the following word classes, including the types of phrase in which they are found. Give an example of each, with the relevant word underlined, as in the example above.

> Use the _Glossary_ at the back of this book if you get stuck.

(a) _modal auxiliary_   (c) _intransitive verb_   (e) _superlative adjective_
(b) _adverb_   (d) _co-ordinating conjunction_   (f) _proper noun_

Marked and unmarked word order

Foregrounding

Task C3 – Word order

Where the word order of English is unmarked, adjectives come before nouns and the order of clause elements is: subject, predicate, object. Novelists and poets may change word order to foreground a particular aspect of the sentence, or in order to create a rhyme.

Identify the changes to word order in the three examples, taken from the poems found in Tasks B6 and C1. Rewrite each example and explain the changes that have taken place, using grammatical terminology.

(a) *To give at evening pale*
Unto the nightingale,
That thou mayst listen the cold dews among?

(b) *All mimsy were the borogoves*

(c) *Long time the manxome foe he sought –*
So rested he by the Tumtum tree,

Another important aspect of English word order is the use of passive constructions.

Active and passive

Look at the sentences below. Identify those that are active and those that are passive.

> Active sentences have actors as subjects.

(d) The clock stopped.
(e) William switched on the television.
(f) The traffic had been stopped by the policeman.
(g) The vicar had begun the service with a hymn.
(h) The ducks were swimming on the lake.
(i) The silence was broken.
(j) The children were happy.
(k) The policeman stopped the traffic.

Intra-sentential cohesion

Task C4 – Cohesion within sentences

We describe the connections between words within a sentence as intra-sentential cohesion. This can be created in a number of ways, through *reference, substitution, ellipsis, conjunction* and *lexical cohesion* (which involves the semantic relations dealt with in Task B2). Using these devices, cohesion can also be created between sentences at a textual level. This will be looked at in Section D of the audit.

Find one example of each of the following intra-sentential cohesive devices in either of the two sentences below, taken from Jane Austen's *Persuasion*.

anaphoric reference   *ellipsis*   *conjunction*   *lexical cohesion*

> Look for items that help the sentence hang together.

(a) *The time now approached for Lady Russell's return; the day was even fixed, and Anne, being engaged to join her as soon as she was resettled, was looking forward to an early removal to Kellynch, and beginning to think how her own comfort was likely to be affected by it.*

(CHAPTER 11)

(b) *Lady Russell had only to listen composedly, and wish them happy; but internally her heart revelled in angry pleasure, in pleased contempt, that a man who at twenty-three had seemed to understand somewhat of the value of an Anne Elliot, should eight years afterwards, be charmed by a Louisa Musgrove.*

(CHAPTER 13)

Task C5 – Complex sentences

Sentences come in three main types – *simple, compound* and *complex* – depending on the type and number of clauses within them.

Determine which of the following sentences are simple sentences, which are compound and which are complex, and indicate the number and type of clause(s) they contain.

e.g. *But as I pushed open the stiff door*   subordinate clause
and
caught my first glimpse of the pool   subordinate clause
it seemed like a dream come true.   main clause

> Remember that a clause should contain a verb.

Contains three clauses: two subordinate clauses followed by the main clause. It is therefore a complex sentence.

(a) We went inside school for the register.
(b) When we got there, we went into a room.
(c) Mark was really excited because they were going on a plane.
(d) I twisted the rusty key in the lock; it snapped against my skin as I placed the rubber band which it was attached to over my wrist.
(e) We went inside school for the register and the coach came and we got on the coach.
(f) Through the glimmering glass windows I could see the cool, clean water sparkle in the morning sun.

....

Task C6 – Co-ordination and subordination

Children's phrases and sentences become longer and more complex as they develop as writers. Complexity is developed through the use of a variety of clause and sentence types.

> There is a distinction here between complex and complexity. We have seen that 'complex' has a specific meaning in relation to sentences. Here we are looking at complexity in its general sense, meaning elaborate.

Match the syntactic labels to the underlined sections in the examples.

prepositional phrase   subordinate clause   main clause   adjectival phrase
verb phrase   noun phrase   finite clause   relative clause

(a) There was a beautiful, white, shiny palace.
(b) This was going to be fun.
(c) We went into a room.
(d) I placed the rubber band, which it was attached to, over my wrist.
(e) The clanking that was coming from below me suddenly stopped.
(f) His mum and dad were quite rich.
(g) When we got there we went into a room.
(h) Mark was really excited because they were going on a plane.

> Note: You may use labels more than once and some of the examples have two appropriate labels.

Examine the three texts on page 16 whose writers demonstrate syntactic development. Comment on the progression of:

(i) the complexity of phrases – nominal, verbal, adjectival, prepositional and adverbial.

> A phrase is a group of words with a head word whose word class distinguishes the group – a noun phrase contains a noun as head.

(j) the development of syntactic complexity, referring to the variety of clause and sentence types and the degree of subordination or co-ordination which characterizes the texts: main and subordinate clauses, simple, compound and complex sentences.

Simple, compound and complex sentences

Sentence complexity

Syntax

Phrase and clause complexity

TEXT 1: *A School Trip*

we went inside school for the register and the coach came and we got on the coach and when we got there we went into a room and put the bags on a hanger and then we went into a room and we had milk and we went to the lake and we played a game and we went back to the room and we went to see the swans and the baby swans as well and we went to the hide-out and we saw the birds and it was good then we went back to school and we went home

TEXT 2: *Chapter 1 – Mark*

Mark was a pretty normal boy but he was never really happy (like most people are). His mum and dad were quite rich and they bought him lots of things to play with. But however many toys he got he always wanted more. He lived in Birmingham so he didn't go to the seaside much. Two weeks later his mum and dad decided to go to the South of France for a week. Mark was really excited because they were going on a plane.

The first day they were there they unpacked their bags and went down to the sea. The sea was warmer than in England and Mark was swimming in it. He dived down and got caught in a sudden little whirlpool. Down he went very quickly, he tried to scream but instead he got a mouth full of water. Suddenly the whirlpool stopped and Mark was lying on the sea bed. He looked up and there was a beautiful, white shiny palace! Also in shiny blue and red letters it said THE WORLD FROM UNDER THE SEA.

TEXT 3: *Take a Swim with Danger*

I was totally fed up, so I decided it was time to take advantage of the hotel swimming pool. Moments before I had rung my two best friends Jade and Danielle and they had agreed they would meet me in the pool. I could still hear my brother's screams ringing in my head. The clanking that was coming from below me suddenly stopped, and, with a single shudder the lift doors opened. I stepped inside, the doors closed, I was alone in he lift and, as I cascaded down many floors a thought entered my head. This was going to be fun.

When I got out of the lift on the ground floor, I made my way towards the reception desk, and then headed down a short corridor towards the hotel swimming pool. I registered in and took a towel and, through the glimmering glass windows I could see the cool clean water sparkle in the morning sun.

I walked towards the ladies' changing rooms. I swiftly got undressed and placed my clothes in the dark and damp locker. I twisted the rusty key in the lock; it snapped against my skin as I placed the rubber band which it was attached to over my wrist. My feet slapped on the surprisingly dry floor as I ran towards the pool. But as I pushed open the stiff doors and caught my first glimpse of the pool it seemed like a dream come true.

Task C7 – Standard and non-standard grammar

Although languages are constantly changing, and have 'rules' that are in reality matters of convention and agreement, it is generally accepted that, in its written form, what we call standard English is a version of the language that is less tolerant of dialect and non-standard usage. In short, in standard written English, if we stray from the norms, we create errors.

Standard English

Standard written English

Identify the error in each of the following examples. Write out the sentence correctly.

Identify the type of error in each case, using technical language.

(a) The childrens party will take place in the Dining Hall today between 2.00 and 3.30 p.m.

(b) The incidences of speeding recorded over the past year on this stretch of road has increased, if we compare the statistics with the previous 12 months.

(c) 'You should of seen him run the 200 metres,' said Mary to her friend Ann at the school's Sports Day.

(d) 'The pupils were in the classroom at lunch time, when they know there not allowed to be in the form rooms.'

(e) However, things did not go as easy as expected.

(f) Team membership allows pupils to develop confidence and show a sense of pride in the community in which they have become a part of.

(g) I bought a Jaguar. It was the best car I had ever drove.

(h) The test was more easier than I expected.

(i) I had hoped for less interruptions.

Agreement

In the following examples grammatical agreement of subject and predicate (verb) is focused on. Choose the correct form of the verb to match the subject from the choices in brackets.

(j) Throughout history schools, and the way they teach pupils, (has/have) changed.

(k) There (is/are/was/were) three stages of school: infant, junior and secondary.

(l) On the other hand there (was/were) many positive aspects to my education.

(m) Their basic skills of writing (needs/need) to be worked on.

(n) The songs which we listened to on the radio (was/were) relaxing.

Adjective or adverb?

Choose the correct adjective or adverb in the following sentences:

(o) I saw him quite (clear/clearly) through my binoculars.

(p) The girls did very (good/well) in the netball tournament.

(q) He drives (dangerous/dangerously) on the motorway.

Non-Standard dialect
Differences in grammar and vocabulary

Non-standard English dialects vary from standard English in terms of their grammar, lexis and phonology. You need to be able to identify the differences in grammar and vocabulary between standard and non-standard English.

The passage that follows on page 18 is a transcript of some spoken non-standard English. It is taken from Hughes and Trudgill's (1979) *English Accents and Dialects* and is an example of a West Midlands dialect.

(r) After reading the text, identify and list the features of non-standard grammar and vocabulary found in the dialect. Relate them to examples from the text. Try to use technical grammatical language in your description.

There are differences relating to tense, person and use of negatives, for example.

[Note: dots (...) between phrases indicate the interviewer's turns in the conversation. These have been removed to leave the interviewee's speech. In addition, the extract has been edited from the original, to shorten it.]

And I said to my wife, I says, er, are you coming to bed? Her says, no, I'm going to see the finish of this. I says, all right then, goodnight, and I went up to bed. ... I used to be keen. I used to be a good footballer myself ... yeh ... Goodyears and all those, you know, they was high class teams, I mean you played for the honour then, I mean, you didn't get nothing out of it ... Well Dave Mackay was on the wireless this morning before I come out, you know, and they was interviewing him, the reporter, and he said he couldn't understand it why they couldn't score at home.

... Well er they never spent no money but they got local talent ... they got a lot of local talent what come up ... you know, like, like ... out of the amateur sides.

> Bear in mind that this is a transcript of speech, not a piece of writing.

Task C8 – Grammar and punctuation

Syntactic units and prosodic features

Punctuation has two functions in writing: it reflects the grammatical or syntactic units in sentences and it reflects the prosodic features of speech.

Comma

In the following sentences *commas* are used for different purposes. Explain the grammatical function of the *commas*, or lack of them, in each case.

(a) My diet excludes butter, chips, ice cream and chocolate.
(b) Fat, especially saturated fat, should be carefully controlled.
(c) When low fat margarine is used, it should be sparingly applied.
(d) Vegetables, which can be eaten freely, contain many essential vitamins.
(e) Desserts that have a higher sugar content should be avoided.

Colon and semi-colon

In the following sentences an underscore (_) is used to indicate the presence of a *colon* or *semi-colon*. Decide which of these marks is most appropriate in each case.

(f) Debbie dropped her bag and out spilled the contents_ a large bunch of keys_ her husband's wallet that she had been asked to keep_ a calculator for the shopping and a rather crumpled handkerchief.
(g) They talked all day without mentioning the one topic on their minds_ the robbery.
(h) I once had a Jaguar car_ it was the best I had ever driven.
(i) The sun shone_ the birds sang_ I was happy.

Apostrophe

Apostrophes have been omitted from some of the following sentences. Add them where and if necessary and explain the rule or reasoning behind your choice.

(j) The childrens teacher arrived in the classroom to begin the day.
(k) Womens fiction is a popular area of study on degree courses.
(l) Ill be coming home at 4.30 today.
(m) The dogs dinner looked very unappetizing to me.
(n) We were completely exhausted at the end of our days exploration.
(o) Common misuses are exemplified in the following pairs of sentences. Identify the correct usage and explain the problems with the incorrect ones.

Bill's Mum gave me a lift to school.	Bills Mum gave me a lift to school.
The trains brakes failed.	The train's brakes failed.
Its a nice day today.	It's a nice day today
The dog ate it's dinner.	The dog ate its dinner.
The window's are looking dirty.	The windows are looking dirty.

What has gone wrong here?

Section D:

The textual system of written language

Inter-sentential cohesion

Cohesive tie

Task D1 – Textual cohesion

Intra-sentential cohesion (cohesion within sentences) was covered in Task C5. This section focuses on inter-sentential cohesion, which uses the same kinds of links – *reference, substitution, ellipsis, conjunction* and *lexical cohesion* – although these are now made between words, sentences and paragraphs at a textual level.

In the feedback section, each of the superscript numbered items in the extract below is assigned to one of the following categories of cohesive tie. Read the extract from *Pride and Prejudice* carefully and identify one example of each of the following categories of textual cohesion.

(a) *reference* (c) *ellipsis* (e) *lexical cohesion*
(b) *substitution* (d) *conjunction*

Then:

(f) find the cohesive tie which stretches over the greatest distance in the extract.

To the little town of Lambton, the scene of Mrs Gardiner's former residence, and where she had lately learned that some acquaintance still remained, **they bent their steps**[1], *after having seen all the principal wonders of the country; and within five miles of* **Lambton**[2], *Elizabeth found from* **her aunt**[3], *that Pemberley was situated.* **It**[4] *was not in their direct road, nor more than a mile or two out of* **it**[5]. *In talking over* **their route**[6] *the evening before*[7], *Mrs Gardiner expressed an inclination to see* **the place**[8] *again. Mr Gardiner* **declared his willingness**[9], *and Elizabeth was applied to for her* **approbation**[10].*

'My love, should not you like to see **a place**[11] *of which you have heard so much?' said her aunt. 'A place too, with which so many of your acquaintance are connected. Wickham passed all his youth* **there**[12]*, you know.'*

Elizabeth was distressed. She felt that she had no business at Pemberley, and was obliged to assume a **disinclination**[13] *for seeing it. She must own that she was tired of great houses; after going over* **so many**[14]*, she had no pleasure in fine carpets or satin curtains.*

Mrs Gardiner abused her stupidity. 'If it were merely a **fine**[15] *house richly furnished', said she, 'I should not care about it myself; but the grounds are delightful. They have some of the finest woods in the country.'*

Elizabeth said no more – but her mind could **not acquiesce**[16]*. The possibility of meeting Mr Darcy, while viewing the place, instantly occurred. It would be dreadful! She blushed at* **the very idea**[17]*; and thought it would be better to speak openly to her aunt, than to run* **such**[18] *a risk. But against* **this**[19]*, there were objections; and she finally resolved that it could be the last resource, if her private enquiries as to the absence of the family, were unfavourably answered.*

Some of the highlighted cohesive items tie with each other; for others, you will have to identify the word(s) in the text.

Accordingly[20], *when she retired at night, she asked the chambermaid whether Pemberley were not a very fine place, what was the name of its proprietor, and with no little alarm, whether the family were down for the summer. A most welcome negative followed **the last question**[21] – and her alarms being now removed, she was at leisure to feel a great deal of curiosity to see the house herself; and when **the subject**[22] was revived the next morning, and she was **again applied to**[23], could readily answer, and with a proper air of indifference, that she had **not really any dislike to the scheme**[24].*

*To Pemberley, **therefore**[25], **they**[26] were to go.*

CHAPTER 43

*Elizabeth, as they drove along, watched for the first appearance of **Pemberley Woods**[27] with some **perturbation**[28]; and when at length they turned in at the lodge, her **spirits were in a high flutter**[29].*

Form

Task D2 – Text structure, form and genre

Read the following poems and extracts, all but the last by Keats. Each has been selected as an example of a particular poetic form, apart from one, where the focus is on the arrangement of the lines. Identify the form in each case.

(a) **To Sleep**

O soft embalmer of the still midnight,
Shutting, with careful fingers and benign,
Our gloom-pleased eyes, embowered from the light,
Enshaded in forgetfulness divine:
O soothest Sleep! if so it please thee, close
In midst of this thine hymn, my willing eyes,
Or wait the 'Amen', ere thy poppy throws
Around my bed its lulling charities.
Then save me, or the passèd day will shine
Upon my pillow, breeding many woes;
Save me from curious conscience, that still hoards
Its strength for darkness, burrowing like a mole;
Turn the key deftly in the oilèd wards,
And seal the hushèd casket of my soul.

(b) **La Belle Dame sans Merci (extract)**

I
O what can ail thee, knight-at-arms,
Alone and palely loitering?
The sedge has withered from the lake,
And no birds sing.

II
O what can ail thee, knight-at-arms,
So haggard and so woe-begone?
The squirrel's granary is full,
And the harvest's done.

III
I see a lily on thy brow,
With anguish moist and fever-dew,
And on thy cheeks a fading rose
Fast withereth too.

IV
I met a lady in the meads,
Full beautiful – a faery's child,
Her hair was long, her foot was light,
And her eyes were wild.

(c) 'The Gothic looks solemn'

The Gothic looks solemn –
The plain Doric column
Supports an old Bishop and crosier;
The mouldering arch,
Shaded o'er by larch
Stands next door to Wilson the Hosier.

Vice – that is, by turns –
O'er pale faces mourns
The black-tassled trencher and common hat;
The chantry boy sings,
The steeple bell rings,
And as for the Chancellor – dominat.

There are plenty of trees,
And plenty of ease,
And plenty of fat deer for parsons;
And when it is venison,
Short is the benison –
Then each on a leg or thigh fastens.

> Examples (c) and (d)
> are not so easily tied
> to a form. What do
> they remind you of?

(d) 'Two or three posies'

Two or three posies
With two or three simples –
Two or three noses
With two or three pimples –
Two or three wise men
And two or three ninnies –
Two or three purses
And two or three guineas –

(LINES 1–8)

(e) Lamia

Part I
Upon a time before the faery broods
Drove Nymph and Satyr from the prosperous woods,
Before King Oberon's bright diadem,
Sceptre, and mantle, clasped with dewy gem,
Frighted away the Dryads and the Fauns
From rushes green, and brakes, and cowslipped lawns,
The ever-smitten Hermes empty left
His golden throne, bent warm on amorous theft:

(f) 'Morning'

Blackbirds in tree tops
Cool dew on fresh summer grass
Warm rays of morning.

Genre produces structural effects because each genre has a different purpose and those communicative purposes constrain the form. The use of spoken and written genres requires knowledge of the conventions associated with them. When we visit the doctor, for example, our language is constrained by the situation and our role within it. Language is governed by its social and generic context.

(g) Comment on the conventional features that characterize the two genres below in terms of their structure and purpose:

- a junk mail letter trying to persuade you to buy a particular service. The authentic text is included below (it has been made anonymous by changing names of locations and the company)

- the blurb on the back of a novel. Look at the back of three novels you own and comment on the regular features of this genre

> Think about the text's regular structural features.

> Consider visual effects as well as linguistic ones.

> Use the following questions to help:
>
> - How does the genre generally open? What is its purpose?
>
> - What kinds of sentence characterize the body of the text and what is their purpose?
>
> - How does it generally close?
>
> - Does it use any specialized vocabulary?
>
> - What presentational devices, such as paragraphing, bullets, layout and use of fonts do the written texts use?

Dear Mrs Jones

Take a Short Break This Summer

As a valued guest of one of these three splendid hotels – 'The Imperial' in Xtown, 'The Majestic' in Ytown and 'The Splendid' in Ztown, we are delighted to offer you an opportunity to indulge in a fabulous Summer Break being offered by the hotels' new owners – the Olympus Hotel Group.

The Olympus Hotel Group comprises a selection of Victorian and Georgian hotels situated in superb locations in the country, city or by the seaside, offering superb cuisine and plenty of things to see and do, at:

* Palace Hotel Golf and Country Club in Derbyshire – a four star Georgian hotel set in 26 acres with its own 18 hole championship golf course and leisure club.

* Princess Hotel in Scarborough – a Victorian hotel overlooking the magnificent bay with views of the harbour and castle.

Special Offer!

If you take your break by 27 August 1998, you will pay only **£39.00 Bed and Breakfast** per person – a great saving. Book now!

In addition, any couple staying a minimum of three nights will receive a free luxury hamper!

It's simple to book. Call our freephone number on 0000 222222 where we will be happy to help.

We look forward to welcoming you this summer.

Yours sincerely

Managing Director

CALL FREE on 0000 222222 to book your Summer Break.

Section E:

Language as a social, cultural and historical phenomenon

Written and spoken English

Similarities and differences between speech and writing

Task E1 – Written versus spoken English

This task involves the description of the distinctive features of speech and writing. Similarities and differences will depend on the types of speech and writing compared. A scripted speech will have many of the features of writing and a piece of writing from a child will have many of the features of speech. An e-mail message to a friend will be hardly distinguishable, in its informality and colloquial usage, from a telephone conversation with her. But, if we are to help pupils move from writing with speech-like features to standard written English and well-written prose, we need to be able to isolate the features that distinguish each form. Let us take a fairly informal conversation between a teenager and an adult about work possibilities (Text A) and a section of narrative with some reported speech (Text B).

TEXT A

Features of speech

(   ) indicates overlap with previous speaker.

A: *Right. So, you're fourteen now, are you taking exams and things at school?*
B: *Erm yeah, some things like maths.*
A: *Oh right.*
B: *I've got one coming up soon.*
A: *Sorry, say that again.*
B: *I've got one coming up soon-*
A: *Have you?*
B: *Maths.*
A: *Are you going to be any good at that then?*
B: *Erm probably.*
A: *Yeah?*
B: *Okay, average.*
A: *That's all right then. So what are your favourite subjects at school then?*
B: *I like design and communication.*
A: *Right.*
B: *Erm drama.*
A: *Mm.*
B: *Er maths is okay.*
A: *Maths okay.*
B: *Mm.*
A: *As long as you can count up and, like, do the basics it's all right, isn't it? Unless you want to do something with maths, it's just- as long as the basics are there you're okay. So what do you want to do when you leave school, have you thought about that?*
B: *Be a veterinary nurse.*
A: *A veterinary nurse? Oh are you practising on all your animals, are you? Are you watching that Animal Watch thing on-*
B: *Yeah.*
A: *That's quite good, isn't it? The trouble is I get so up- you know, I get so upset when they bring in animals like that. I couldn't be a vet 'cause I'd be crying all the time. So you can handle that, can you?*
B: *Think so.*
A: *(All right.) Do you go and er help out at other places with animals?*
B: *Erm well I use- I went on a course-*

> Sentence length is one obvious difference, with many short utterances, but there are many other features of speech to identify.

A: Uh huh.

B: (Helping) with horses and learned all about them and how to clean them out and things like that.

A: Oh, that's good. You've got to have a bit of experience, haven't you? S- it takes a long time, doesn't it, you've got to become a doctor then a vet, haven't you? You've got to go through lots of college and take lots of exams and all of that sort of stuff, haven't you? So, you're quite prepared to do that, are you?

B: Yeah-

A: Going to work hard for it? Good. Right. Anything you want to ask me?

B: No-

Text B

A shadow fell over my T-bar sandals and I looked up to see Anita Rutter staring at me through squinted eyes ringed in bright blue eyeshadow. She broke off a twig from our privet hedge and thrust it under my nose, pointing at a part of the branch where the leaves were not their usual straight darts but were rolled up in on themselves, neat and packaged as school dinner sandwiches. 'See them leaves?' She carefully unrolled one of them: it came away slowly like sticky tape, to reveal a sprinkling of tiny black eggs. 'Butterflies' eggs, them is. They roll up the leaf to hide them, see.'

She stripped all the leaves off the twig in one movement and smelled her fingers, before flicking the naked branch at my ankles. It stung but I did not pull my legs back. I knew this was a test.

'What you got?'

I held out my crumpled bag of stolen sweets. She peered inside disdainfully, then snatched the bag off me and began walking away as she ate. I watched her go, confused. I could still hear my parents talking inside, their voices now calmer, conciliatory. Anita stopped momentarily, shouting over her shoulder, 'Yow coming then?'

It was the first day of the long summer holidays and I had six whole weeks which I could waste or taste. So I got up and followed her without a word.

I was happy to follow her a respectable few paces behind, knowing that I was privileged to be in her company. Anita was the undisputed 'cock' of our yard, maybe that should have been hen, but her foghorn voice, foul mouth, and proficiency at lassoing victims with her frayed skipping rope indicated she was carrying enough testosterone around to earn the title. She ruled over all the kids in the yard with a mixture of pre-pubescent feminine wiles, pouting, sulking, clumsy cack-handed flirting and unsettling mood swings which would often end in minor violence. She had the face of a pissed-off cherub, huge green eyes, blonde hair, a curling mouth with slightly too many teeth and a brown birthmark under one eye which when she was angry, which was often, seemed to throb and glow like a lump of Superman's kryptonite.

(FROM: MEERA SYAL (1997) *ANITA AND ME*. FLAMINGO, PP. 38–9)

(a) The following statements describe features of written and spoken text. Divide them into two groups, according to whether you think they describe speech or writing, using Texts A and B for reference.

uses tag questions
uses a range of sentence and clause types
uses long complex noun phrases
uses cohesion to avoid repetition
uses truncated sentences

uses hesitation markers
uses core vocabulary, rather than a broad range
sentences are mainly compound and simple
has a range of subordinating conjunctions
uses few signals of interaction

....

Task E2 – Multilingualism and language variety

Multilingualism

Language variety

Britain is a multilingual country, with a wide variety of languages and dialects being spoken. In order to reflect this variety, we need to develop a language that reflects our understanding and knowledge.

Match the following terms to their definitions:

1. *creole*   5. *linguistic cognate*
2. *heritage language*   6. *pidgin*
3. *accent*   7. *dialect*
4. *common underlying proficiency*   8. *bilingualism*

(a) The way we pronounce words, according to our geographical and, sometimes, social position.
(b) The ability to use two languages.
(c) Involves the cognitive relationship between two languages, knowledge of which is used by bilinguals.
(d) A language that develops from a mixture of languages.
(e) A social or regional variety of language, characterized by particular grammatical and lexical features: Cockney, Glaswegian, standard English.
(f) The language regarded as the native, home or ancestral language, which may be indigenous, such as Welsh or Gaelic.
(g) Words related to each other by a semantic bond. In bilingual speakers they are words that are used to relate new words in one language to known words in the other language.
(h) A mixture of two languages. It is not the speaker's native language, but is used and developed in order for two speakers, who do not share a common language, to communicate.

....

Task E3 – Historical changes in English

Historical change

Old English and Modern English

Modern English exists as a result of a long, and continuing, evolution. English has changed in many ways as it has developed from Old English to Modern English.

(a) Seven different types of language change are listed below. Choose three from the seven. Describe the changes, giving an example for each.

Phonological change

e.g.   *phonological change*: OE word *tima* – first vowel pronounced /iː/, and Modern English word *time* – vowel pronounced /aɪ/. Long vowels have changed to diphthongs.

1. *orthographical change*
2. *changes in letter forms and the alphabet*
3. *changes in grammar and word order*
4. *morphological change*
5. *changes in punctuation*
6. *changes in vocabulary, including introductions and borrowings*
7. *semantic change*

Words have changed in meaning over time and become obsolete.

(b) Choose five of the emboldened words in this extract from *Julius Caesar* and comment on the changes in meaning and usage.

> *ANTONY*
> *O, pardon me, **thou** bleeding piece of earth,*
> *That I am meek and gentle with these butchers.*
> *Thou art the ruins of the noblest man*
> *That ever lived in the tide of times.*
> *Woe to the hand that shed this costly blood!*
> *Over **thy** wounds now do I prophesy –*
> *Which like dumb mouths do ope their ruby lips.*
> *To beg the voice and utterance of my tongue –*
> *A curse shall light upon the limbs of men;*
> *Domestic fury and fierce civil strife*
> *Shall **cumber** all the parts of Italy;*
> *Blood and destruction shall be so in use,*
> *And dreadful objects so familiar,*
> *That mothers shall but smile when they behold*
> *Their infants **quartered** with the hands of war,*
> *All pity choked with custom of **fell** deeds;*
> *And Caesar's spirit, **ranging** for revenge.*
> *With Ate by his side, come hot from hell,*
> *Shall in these confines with a monarch's voice*
> *Cry havoc and **let slip** the dogs of war,*
> *That this foul deed shall smell above the earth*
> *With carrion men, groaning for burial.*
>
> ***Post** back with speed, and tell him what hath **chanced**.*
> *Here is a mourning Rome, a dangerous Rome,*
> *No Rome of safety for Octavius yet.*
> ***Hie hence**, and tell him so. Yet stay awhile;*
> ***Thou shalt** not back till I have borne this **corse***
> *Into the market-place; there shall I **try**,*
> *In my oration, how the people take*
> *The cruel **issue** of these bloody men;*
> *According to the which, thou **shalt discourse***
> *To young Octavius of the state of things.*
> *Lend me your hand.*

(III.I – LINES 255–297)

> It will be difficult to distinguish between language change and poetic diction in some cases, but poetic diction itself uses archaisms.

Section F:

Knowledge about texts and critical approaches to them

Task F1 – Response to fiction and non-fiction

Critical evaluation and the formation of judgements in response to text involve analytical skills of reading, and speaking and listening. These are stated in the National Curriculum for English, although not in a discrete section.

(a) Divide the skills listed below into those that you think could be developed through the teaching of reading and those that could be developed through speaking and listening.

- *extract meaning beyond the literal through explanation of language and style*

- *articulate informed personal opinions*
- *discuss alternative interpretations*
- *analyse and engage with ideas, themes and language*
- *select relevant information and evidence objectively*
- *consider how texts are changed when adapted to different media*

Task F2 – Presentation of information and ideas

Contextual features

The presentation of information and ideas in fiction and non-fiction is dependent on context. The context involves audience and purpose and the interplay between these and the writer or speaker. Context also involves the writer's position, which is a complex situation involving the influences of biography – social situation, personal ideologies and philosophies, background, influences – and their contribution to the point of view adopted by the writer.

Text type

(a) The table below gives six text types. Each is described in terms of its contextual influences and the effects of these on the textual presentation of ideas. Match these to the seven examples listed here:

- BBC Television's children's news programme, *Newsround*
- A television advertisement for an alcoholic drink
- A recipe
- Jean Rhys's *Wide Sargasso Sea*
- *Little Red Riding Hood* – children's fairy tale
- A feature article in a teenage magazine for girls
- A section in a Haynes's car manual, outlining the procedure for inspecting and renewing the rear brake linings on a car

TEXT TYPE	EFFECT OF CONTEXT ON PRESENTATION OF IDEAS
A	ideas of cause and effect are logically connected and good and evil are presented in clearly defined characters; the issue of obedience to parents is reinforced whilst also being presented in an entertaining story, which creates suspense, evil and resolution of evil; use of illustration.
B	the effect is a discursive, informal style with a sometimes conspiratorial, sometimes sarcastic tone.
C	uses effects such as humour, self-endorsement, identification; plays on viewer's ideal self image.
D	the reader is given many viewpoints; the author explores (and makes the reader explore) the positions of each of the characters, making this a psychological exploration of character and interaction.
E	a step-by-step procedure is given to be followed; use of instructions for action and use of diagrams or pictures to support text.
F	ideas presented clearly, graphically, concisely, informatively and educationally; technical terms explained and defined.

Narration

The next task involves thinking about techniques of narrative.

(b) Read the extract below. Comment on the effect of tense changes in the emboldened sections of this extract from the end of Jean Rhys's *Wide Sargasso Sea*.

> ***That was the third time I had my dream, and it ended. I know now that the flight of steps leads to this room where I lie watching the woman asleep with her head on her arms.*** *In my dream I waited till she began to snore, then I got up, took the keys and let myself out with a candle in my hand. It was easier this time than ever before and I walked as though I were flying.*

All the people who had been staying in the house had gone, for the bedroom doors were shut, but it seemed to me that someone was following me, someone was chasing me, laughing. Sometimes I looked to the right or left but I never looked behind me for I did not want to see that ghost of a woman whom they say haunts this place. I went down the staircase. I went further than I had ever been before. There was someone talking in one of the rooms. I passed it without noise, slowly.

At last I was in the hall where a lamp was burning. I remember that when I came. A lamp and the dark staircase and the veil over my face. They think I don't remember but I do. *There was a door to the right. I opened it and went in. It was a large room with a red carpet and red curtains. Everything else was white. I sat down on a couch to look at it and it seemed sad and cold and empty to me, like a church without an altar. I wished to see it clearly so I lit all the candles, and there were many ...*

... All this I saw and heard in a fraction of a second. And the sky so red. Someone screamed and I thought, Why did I scream? I called 'Tia!' and jumped and woke.

Grace Poole was sitting at the table but she had heard the scream too, for she said, 'What was that?' She got up, came over and looked at me. I lay still, breathing evenly with my eyes shut. 'I must have been dreaming,' she said. Then she went back, not to the table but to her bed. **I waited a long time after I heard her snore, then got up, took the keys and unlocked the door. I was outside holding my candle. Now at last I know why I was brought here and what I have to do. There must have been a draught for the flame flickered and I thought it was out. But I shielded it with my hand and it burned up again to light me along the dark passage.**

> Dots indicate a long continuation of the descriptive passage in the past tense.

Tone

Task F3 – Implication, undertone, bias, assertion and ambiguity

The numerous resources available to writers (and speakers) of fiction and non-fiction have been developed over many years and are reiterated across texts. Effective text is written in a way that has impact and creates the intrigue and involvement so essential for imaginative response.

Choose three of the terms below and, using an example from an extract of text that you know well, describe how its use contributes to the message and impact of the text at that point, or as a whole, in terms of implication, undertone, bias, assertion or ambiguity.

allegory	*bias*	*irony*	*satire*
allusion	*burlesque*	*language choice*	*setting*
ambiguity	*characterization*	*motif*	*symbolism*
analogy	*figurative language*	*paradox*	*theme*
antithesis	*form*	*parody*	
bathos	*imagery*	*pathos*	

> You may add your own terms to these.

Task F4 – Critical approaches

Ways of reading
Interpretation

Critical approaches to literature are not new. Since the early Greek philosophers, critics and writers have been vying to outnumber each other. But the nineteenth and twentieth centuries have seen an increase in approaches to criticism, to such an extent that a single work has spawned a shelf of criticism. Criticism, therefore, cannot be ignored. Each approach emphasizes different ways of reading and interpreting texts and as long as the text, and not the critique, remains at the centre of the reading process, critical approaches will enhance understanding and interpretation.

(a) Match each of the following critical approaches to the definitions below:

(a) *Reader-response theory*   (e) *Structuralism*
(b) *Feminist criticism*   (f) *Psycho-analytical criticism*
(c) *Biographical criticism*   (g) *Post-Structuralism*
(d) *Marxist criticism*   (h) *Stylistics*

1. An approach that involves a sociological, ideological and political reading of text.
2. An approach that involves an examination of the relationship between the biography of the author and the text production or product.
3. The study of aspects of the text, using objective rather than subjective judgements of the contributions of grammar, lexis, rhetoric, semantics, meter and phonology to the meaning of the text.
4. A theory originating from Wolfgang Iser, which describes the relationship between reader, writer and text.
5. The study of texts, film and media, using Saussurean linguistics, particularly in terms of the way language signifies and creates associations.
6. A theory that suggests that texts have multiple and different meanings. The French theorists, Roland Barthes and Jacques Derrida, are particularly influential.
7. An approach that uses the techniques of psychoanalysis to interpret literature.
8. A critical process that examines and interprets literature from a perspective of questioning stereotypes and masculine positions, and examining the positions of women.

(b) Give one example of a text from the following list, and one from your own knowledge, whose interpretation would benefit from one or more of these critical approaches.

George Orwell's *Animal Farm*
Charlotte Bronte's *Jane Eyre*
John Fowles's *The French Lieutenant's Woman*
Alice Walker's *The Color Purple*
Umberto Eco's *The Name of the Rose*
Graham Greene's *Brighton Rock*
A children's fairy tale, such as *Little Red Riding Hood*
The poetry of Dylan Thomas
Gene Kemp's children's story *The Turbulent Term of Tyke Tyler*

Section G:

Knowledge of a range of texts

Task G – Authors and texts
Familiarity with a broad range of texts and authors is important.

(a) Look at the lists of authors under the range of categories on the following pages. You should be able to name one work by each of them, and nine works by Shakespeare.

Drama

SHAKESPEARE
three comedies
three tragedies
three history plays

DRAMA POST-1900
Alan Ayckbourn
Edward Bond
John Osborne
J. B. Priestley
George Bernard Shaw

DRAMA PRE-1900
Aphra Behn
Christopher Marlowe
R. B. Sheridan
Cyril Tourneur

EUROPEAN DRAMA
Bertolt Brecht
Anton Chekhov
Henrik Ibsen
Eugène Ionesco

> For some authors, naming one of their works will be a challenge. At the end of the exercise, you should be able to identify areas for further reading, such as drama before 1900, perhaps.

Fiction

FICTION PRE-1900
Jane Austen
Charlotte Brontë
Emily Brontë
John Bunyan
Wilkie Collins
Daniel Defoe
Charles Dickens
Arthur Conan Doyle
George Eliot
Henry Fielding
Elizabeth Gaskell
Thomas Hardy
Henry James
Mary Shelley
Robert Louis Stevenson
Jonathan Swift
Anthony Trollope
H. G. Wells

FICTION POST-1900
Maya Angelou
Margaret Atwood
Anita Brookner
E. M. Forster
William Golding
Graham Greene
Ernest Hemingway
Kazuo Ishiguro
P. D. James
James Joyce
Jack Kerouac
D. H. Lawrence
Penelope Lively
Ben Okri
George Orwell
Salman Rushdie
Paul Scott
Muriel Spark
Amy Tan
Fay Weldon

> Categories are by no means discrete. Writers such as Arthur Conan Doyle, Thomas Hardy and H. G. Wells published both pre- and post-1900.

Poetry

POETRY PRE-1900
William Blake
(George Gordon) Lord Byron
Geoffrey Chaucer
John Clare
Samuel Taylor Coleridge
John Donne
George Herbert
Andrew Marvell
John Milton

POETRY POST-1900
W. H. Auden
T. S. Eliot
Thom Gunn
Thomas Hardy
Seamus Heaney
Ted Hughes
Philip Larkin
R. S. Thomas
W. B. Yeats

> Thomas Hardy and W. B. Yeats published poems in both the nineteenth and the twentieth centuries.

EUROPEAN LITERATURE
Albert Camus
Fyodor Dostoevsky
Umberto Eco
Gustave Flaubert
Franz Kafka
Milan Kundera
Primo Levi
Alexander Solzhenitsyn
Stendhal
Emile Zola

NON-FICTION
Name two works for each category:
  autobiography
  biography
  journal
  diary
  collections of letters
  travel writing
  other prose

TEXTS BY WRITERS FROM OTHER CULTURES AND FROM MULTICULTURAL BRITAIN
(Can you also assign these writers to the categories above: drama, poetry and fiction pre- or post-1900?)

Chimia Achebe	Ben Okri
John Agard	Michael Ondaatje
Edward Kamau Brathwaite	A. K. Ramanujan
Anita Desai	Jean Rhys
Athol Fugard	Salman Rushdie
Nadine Gordimer	Vikram Seth
Linton Kwesi Johnson	Wole Soyinka
Hanit Kureishi	Meera Syal
V. S. Naipaul	Derek Walcott
Ngugi wa Thiong'o	

FICTION AND COLLECTIONS SPECIFICALLY FOR PUPILS IN SECONDARY SCHOOL
Name five works written in this category.

> There are numerous collections of poetry, for example.

CD-ROMS AND WEBSITES
Name two encyclopaedias on CD-ROM.

Make a list of CD-ROMs that you could use to support English study.

Make a list of useful websites for literary or linguistic study or for improving grammar and other writing and reading skills.

(b) In the list of authors of children's literature, can you find the 'real' children's specialists amongst the other writers?

AUTHORS OF CHILDREN'S LITERATURE?

John Austin	Dick King-Smith
Nina Bawden	Clive King
Margaret Berry	Judith Levi
Betsy Byars	C. S. Lewis
Lewis Carroll	Jack London
Margaret Clark	Jim Martin
Helen Cresswell	Wendy Morgan
Gillian Cross	Jenny Nimmo
Bruce Fraser	Robert O'Brien
Anne Fine	Terry Pratchett
Leon Garfield	Michael Stubbs
Alan Garner	Rosemary Sutcliff
John Gibbons	John Rowe Townsend
Ursula Le Guin	E. B. White
Robert Kaplan	Henry Widdowson
Judith Kerr	Jacqueline Wilson
Gene Kemp	Paul Zindel

(c) Find out what each of the following book awards is given for and the name of a book or author to receive the award recently.

CHILDREN'S BOOK AWARDS	ADULT BOOK AWARDS
Carnegie Medal	The Booker Prize
Kate Greenaway Medal	The Nobel Prize for Literature
Guardian Award	The Whitbread Awards
Smarties Prize	The Somerset Maugham Prize
The Whitbread Awards	Prix Goncourt
	The Pulitzer Prize

> You may have come across other book awards. This is just a selection.

Feedback

Three kinds of feedback

Three kinds of feedback are given:

- **Answer(s)**
- **Feedback** – including explanation and guidance for self-study
- **Action** – advice on what to do to develop your knowledge

Answers

No scoring system is provided for marking the answers, although the audit has been devised in a way that makes this possible, since many of the questions involve matching or inserting single items of information. Devising your own scoring system may help you measure progress, especially if you use the audit more than once over a period of time.

Feedback

This will often extend your knowledge beyond that required to answer the questions; in many cases, the questions are merely starting points leading to complex areas of knowledge. Learning is often best done at the border between difficulty and challenge, and your knowledge is being developed through your response to questions and tasks rather than in a decontextualized way. The questions, answers and feedback represent samples of knowledge. Suggestions for further development are contained in the **Action**.

Action

This gives advice on how to follow up the audit with personal study. Any further study that develops your subject knowledge should be recorded in a 'personal learning record' or profile in a section entitled 'subject knowledge', or you can use the personal learning plan outlined at the back of this book. This will ensure that if you are asked at the end of your training to show evidence of how you have filled gaps and developed your subject knowledge, you will have a record of what you have done. Much of your course will duplicate the action suggested.

Using the layout of the feedback chapter

As with the audit, the columns on either side of the main text provide key information. The left-hand column provides the key words from the main text. You can use this to help you scan to locate a particular piece of information, particularly when revisiting an area to check an answer. The right-hand column provides cross references to related explanations in the feedback and gives you advice about how to apply the subject knowledge to your teaching.

How to approach the feedback

Your first task may well be to mark your answers and assess how well you have done. This, however, is only the first step. Finding out what you do or don't know is important but will probably not give you any major surprises, though it may be important for your tutors. What is more important is to understand the nature of English subject knowledge so that you can apply this knowledge in your teaching. For this reason, it is important to read the feedback carefully alongside your answers to the audit. You will also need to refer back to the questions, particularly where an incorrect answer is due to a misunderstanding.

Having checked your answers, you should read the detailed explanation. The feedback will be most useful where you analyse your answers. Ask yourself the following questions:

1. If your answer was correct, did you know the answer, guess it, or did you use clues given in the question to work it out?

2. If your answer was incorrect, did you misunderstand the question, lack the knowledge or did you mis-apply your knowledge?

Based on your answers to these questions, you will be able to assess the level of further study needed. You will also work out where to pay most careful attention in the feedback. The feedback has been written to be as clear as possible, but some explanations require the use of items of technical vocabulary. A glossary of terms is provided at the back of this book for reference.

> Look at the *Personal Learning Plan* at the back of this book. Keep a record both of areas of success and areas for development.

The purpose of the feedback

The feedback will help you to identify areas of strength and secure knowledge and to identify weaknesses and gaps in knowledge. Having done this, you will then be able to target areas for development. You can develop these areas through further reading and self-study suggested in the **Action**.

The feedback should give you confidence where knowledge is secure, and guidance and development in weaker areas. Early targeting of areas for further development will ensure that any gaps identified are filled through self-study and reading, asking questions in relevant seminars on your course and working with pupils and experienced teachers in schools.

> Record any further development in a progress record.

Note

The International Phonetic Alphabet (IPA) has been used to represent sounds. A table of IPA symbols and the phonemes they represent is provided, with examples, on page 98.

Section A:

Technical terms in English language and literature

Technical terms and metalanguage

Task A – Technical terms

Answers
1(k); 2(p); 3(n); 4(q); 5(o); 6(h); 7(i); 8(d); 9(g); 10(s); 11(b); 12(l); 13(m); 14(t); 15(f); 16(e); 17(r); 18(j); 19(a); 20(c).

Feedback
This is only a small selection of terms from the metalanguage of English language and literature, which is particularly rich in terminology. You cannot be expected to know all the terms, but knowledge and appropriate use of key terms is important. You should aim to assimilate this knowledge and use it in your teaching and assignments during your training. You will then become more confident in its use. A glossary of key terms is provided at the end of this book. Each of the terms featured in this task is explained in some detail below.

> See also terms in Tasks B6, C2, C4 and E2.

> When you introduce new terminology to pupils, remember to provide a clear explanation and to check their understanding.

Adverb

1(k)   Adverbs often end with the suffix *-ly* and can be derived from adjectives, e.g. *gentle, gently*. They modify adjectives and verbs, giving an indication of degree, manner, place, time, duration and frequency,

e.g.   *It was <u>very</u> hot. We drove <u>carefully</u>. I moved <u>back</u>. I saw her <u>yesterday</u>. I saw her <u>briefly</u>. Do you come here <u>often</u>?*

Sentence adverb

Adverbs such as *unfortunately, then, next* and *nevertheless* are used as connectives between sentences, coming in sentence initial position. They can be confused with conjunctions because they perform a similar semantic function.

**Reference
Cohesion**

2(p)   Anaphoric reference is one aspect of cohesion. Cohesion is the process whereby links are made between words within sentences or between sentences. Anaphoric reference creates a tie that refers backwards in the text, as in: *Ben and Mike left Wembley early. <u>They</u> had seen enough.* In this example the pronoun *they* refers back to *Ben and Mike* and the writer avoids repetition of the names.

> See the feedback to Tasks C4 and D1 for a detailed explanation of cohesion.

Allusion

3(n)   Literary allusions create depth of meaning. For example, in Anita Brookner's *Hotel du Lac*, when the heroine takes a trip across a Swiss lake with the male protagonist, Mr. Neville, 'a gull-like bird' flies over the steamer on which they are travelling. This allusion to the albatross in 'The Rime of the Ancient Mariner'

Symbol

provides a symbol of danger and warning.

Morpheme

4(q)   Morphemes are the smallest units of meaning. Free morphemes are words that can stand alone. Bound morphemes are units of meaning that cannot stand alone; they have to be attached to a free morpheme. Prefixes, suffixes and inflections are bound morphemes,

e.g.   *un-, pre-, -ful, -ness, -s, -'s*
in: *unkind, preview, useful, usefulness, dogs, dog's.*

> See the feedback to Task B1 for an explanation of morphology including affixation and compounding.

Cloze procedure

5(o)   Cloze procedure requires readers to replace gaps in a text with appropriate words, using syntactic, semantic and contextual clues provided by the text. Analysis of correct answers and errors can give evidence of the level of comprehension and can be used to assess the variety of reading strategies employed by the child.

6(h) The double negative is a grammatical feature of many dialects and non-standard speech and writing. It is generally regarded as inappropriate in situations where standard written and spoken English are required.

7(i) Ellipsis is another aspect of cohesion. In the example, *I love hamburgers, but hate onions,* the pronoun *I* is omitted from the second clause, although it functions as the subject of both clauses, thereby avoiding repetition.

> See the feedback to Tasks C4 and D1 for more on cohesion.

8(d) The 26 letters of the alphabet are called graphemes. They are the symbols we use for writing, just as phonemes are the sounds produced in speech.

9(g) Homonyms are words that are spelt and sound the same but have different meanings. These words are polysemantic, which means they have more than one meaning, e.g. *bear.* This is a noun, meaning the animal, and a verb, meaning 'to carry'. Punning, ambiguity and complexity of meaning can be created in poetry and prose through the use of homonyms and their connotations. Consider the connotations and meanings of the word *green* in Dylan Thomas's 'Fern Hill'. Ambiguity can usually be resolved by the context, except where it is deliberate.

> For further implications for spelling, read the section on phonology in Chapter 3.

10(s) Wolfgang Iser's work on reader response proposes that the reader is central to the process of constructing meaning. Authors also write with an implied reader in mind, and the reader is involved in a process of becoming that person. This theory suggests that readers are created by writers.

> For more on reader response, see the feedback to Task F4.

12(l) Modal auxiliaries are auxiliary verbs such as *can, may* and *should.* They indicate necessity, willingness and intention and have an important function in writing that expresses judgements or persuades. They are distinct from temporal auxiliaries (also known as primary auxiliaries), such as *have* and *been* in We <u>have been</u> *eating sweets all day,* although both kinds of auxiliary verb come before a main verb. Temporal auxiliaries are formed using the verbs 'to have' and 'to be' and carry information about tense. They can sometimes be confused with main verbs because the verbs 'to have' and 'to be' can also be main verbs – We <u>had</u> *a good time. We <u>were</u> happy.*

13(m) Sawyer, Watson and Adams (1989: 141) say: 'Unfortunately "pathetic fallacy" has tended to be a derogatory term applied to personification striving for very artificial effects. Perhaps, therefore, it ought to be distinguished from genuine symbolic landscapes that serve as a reflection of human emotion or have a metaphysical relationship with human emotions – for example, Tennyson's:

> *The woods decay, the woods decay and fall,*
> *The vapours weep their burthen to the ground*
>
> ('TITHONUS')'

Comprehension

Dialect

Standard English

Ellipsis
Cohesion

Grapheme
Phoneme

Homonym

Implied reader

Modal auxiliary

Pathetic fallacy

Symbol

Post-structuralism	14(t) Post-structuralism grew out of resistance to structuralism and perceived inadequacies in its approach to reading and meaning. Its emergence, in the 1960s, opened up the possibilities of texts having multiple and different meanings. The French theorists, Roland Barthes and Jacques Derrida, are particularly influential. Close reading, deconstruction of the text and understanding the notion of *différence* all contribute to post-structuralist practice. John Fowles's novel *The French Lieutenant's Woman*, published in 1969, is an example of post-structuralist writing.

For more on ways of reading, see the feedback to Task F4.

Register

15(f) *Register* is a term used to describe the language used in a particular situation. We talk about a *legal register* or the *register of advertising*. Register affects and restricts the meaning and choice of words, and some registers even affect the type of voice qualities required. *Once upon a time ...* is a set of words that signals a particular type of text, a situation and a mode of delivery. You will find that, as a teacher, your voice takes on certain qualities and you use particular words in certain settings, such as with pupils in the classroom.

For humorous effect, you could read a newspaper report in the manner of a fairy story to illustrate the concept of register. This was done in the film 'Three Men and a Baby'.

Schwa

16(e) The schwa is a very common vowel sound in English speech. The sound is the same as the *u* in b<u>u</u>g. It occurs in unstressed syllables of words. Consider <u>a</u>bove, cons<u>o</u>n<u>a</u>nt, independ<u>e</u>nt, forw<u>ar</u>d, fam<u>ou</u>s, comf<u>or</u>t and wat<u>er</u>. Not all accents and pronunciations of English will produce /ə/ in the places indicated, but all are examples of words that may contain the schwa. Its occurrence makes these words difficult for pupils to spell because of the range of graphemes used to make the sound; *a, o, e, ar, ou, or* and *er* are used in the words above. The schwa is the cause of spelling difficulties in *-ent, -ant* and *-ence, -ance* words.

Spelling

Awareness of the difficulties posed by the diversity of phoneme-to-grapheme correspondence is important to diagnosing and remedying this particular type of spelling error. See the feedback to Task B5.

Semiotics

17(r) Roland Barthes (1977) and Umberto Eco (1981) are two key figures in the world of semiotics.

Syntax

18(j) Syntax is the study of the grammar of the sentence, particularly word order. It involves knowledge of the arrangement of words, phrases and clauses, and the rules governing these.

Transitive and intransitive

19(a)
20(c) Intransitive verbs have no object, whilst transitive verbs do. Here, the verb *stop* is used both transitively and intransitively:

SUBJECT	PREDICATE	OBJECT	
The train	*stopped.*		Intransitive verb
The policeman	*stopped*	*the traffic.*	Transitive verb

Passive

Intransitive verbs cannot be made passive.

Action

Look carefully through the programmes of study for Key Stages (2*) 3 and 4 of the National Curriculum (and the syllabuses for A level*). Write down any terms you could not explain in the same way that you have for this task. You should be able to use terminology accurately and confidently. Look up the terms and record your learning in a 'personal learning record' or profile. Some excellent reference books are:

* Requirements will relate to the course you are following and age range you are training to teach.

1. For linguistic terminology:

> Crystal, D. (1987) *The Cambridge Encyclopaedia of the English Language.* Cambridge University Press.
> Carter, R.A. (ed.) (1990) *Knowledge about Language and the Curriculum: LINC Reader.* Hodder & Stoughton.

2. For literary terminology:

> Cuddon, J. A. (1992) *The Penguin Dictionary of Literary Terms and Literary Theory* (third edition). Penguin.

3. Literary and linguistic terminology:

> Sawyer, W., Watson, K. and Adams, A. (eds.) (1989) *English Teaching from A-Z.* Open University Press.

4. A glossary of terms for Key Stages 1 and 2 in:

> DfEE (1998) *The National Literacy Strategy.* DfEE.

> Hereafter, record any learning you do as a result of the feedback or action in this chapter in your *Personal Learning Plan.*

Section B:

The lexical system of spoken and written language

Task B1 – Morphology and semantics

Morphemes

Answers

The table below shows the number and types of morphemes in each of the words.

	Number of morphemes	Derivational prefix	Base/ Free morpheme	Derivational suffix	Inflectional suffix
a	3	con-	clud		-ed (past tense)
b	1		boat		
c	2	super-	market		
d	3	hyper-	activ	-ity	
e	2		quick		-est (superlative)
f	3	re-	vert		-s (third person)
g	2		black + bird		
h	2	un-	tie		

This table shows the meanings of prefixes and suffixes, with examples.

Prefix and suffix meanings

	Prefix/suffix	Meaning	Example(s)
i	con-	with	consult
j	sub-	under	submarine
k	infra-	below	infrastructure
l	inter-	between	intervene
m	-or	doer; one who does something	doctor
n	-oid	like	cuboid
o	dis-	apart; not	disentangle; dissatisfied
p	dys-	bad	dysfunctional; dystopia

Morpheme

Feedback

The structure of English words leads us to the study of morphology. The unit that is central to the study of morphology is the morpheme. A morpheme is defined simply as the smallest unit of meaning. The word *boat*, for example, consists of a single unit of meaning, whereas *boats* consists of two: the item *boat* and the fact that it is plural, shown by the plural morpheme *-s*.

> Three key aspects of morphology are the bases or stems of words, affixes, and the process of compounding.

Free and bound morphemes

Lexeme and base

Morphemes are either free or bound. Free morphemes are units that are freestanding words, such as *boat*. Bound morphemes are those which cannot be freestanding, such as *con-* and *-ed* in **con**clud**ed**. Many Greek and Latin bases that make up English words, such as *clud* in *concluded*, are not freestanding, so we need to make a distinction between lexeme (word) and base.

Prefix, suffix and base

The morphemes that make up English words can be categorized more specifically as prefixes, suffixes and bases, prefixes being added to the front of the base and suffixes added to the end, as in *con-clud-ed*. In this word the Latin prefix *con-*, meaning 'together' is added to the Latin base *clud*, meaning 'shut', and the past tense verbal suffix *-ed* is added to the end.

> We can see that some of the literal meaning of the parts contributes to the meaning of the word.

Derivation and inflection

Prefixes and suffixes can be collectively described as affixes. Affixes can be derivational or inflectional. Derivational affixes can be prefixes or suffixes in English, and can be simply defined as word-forming affixes. They are the prefixes and suffixes that can be used to derive more words from base words. For example, if we take the base *happi*, further words can be derived from it by adding prefixes and suffixes:

DERIVATIONAL PREFIX	BASE	DERIVATIONAL SUFFIX
un-	happi happi	-ness -ly

Comparative and superlative

Inflectional suffixes are those that give grammatical information, such as tense or number, as in *concluded or reverts*. Comparative and superlative suffixes are also inflections:

> Inflections are always found at the end of words in English.

BASE	INFLECTIONAL SUFFIX
happi happi sit	-er -est -s

Compound

Where two free morphemes are joined together, we describe the resulting word as a compound. There are many of these in English. Some are hyphenated, some are completely joined, some can be used either way and some are variable.

e.g.   *blackbird, honeybee, jailbreak*   (completely joined)
      jack-knife, spoon-feed, heat-resistant   (hyphenated)
      mini-skirt, miniskirt; newly-wed, newlywed   (hyphenated or joined)
      new born, new-born, newborn   (variable)

Word boundaries

Because word boundaries are unclear in speech, compound words cause particular problems for writers. For example, writers may split words that should be kept together, such as *owner ship* for *ownership*, or may join words that should be separate: *aswell* and *alot* for *as well* and *a lot*. Prefixes and suffixes can cause similar problems, with writers treating these bound morphemes as freestanding: *hope full* or *pre view*. In the case of *hope full*, the writer is confusing the word *full* with the suffix *-ful*.

> As teachers, you may come across amusing 'oronyms' where sound is divided unsuccessfully into words. I came across *axe dent* for *accident*. Stephen Pinker (1994: 160) cites *Pencil Vanea* for *Pennsylvania*.

The tables below show some common Latin and Greek prefixes and suffixes and their meanings.

Latin and Greek prefixes and suffixes

Meanings

Prefix (Latin)	Meaning	Suffix (Latin)	Meaning/function
ab-, a-	away, from	-acity	quality of being inclined to
ad-, ac-	to, toward	-an, -ian	pertaining to
ambi-	both, around	-ant	adjective forming suffix
circum-	around	-ary, -arium	connected with
ex-, e-	out, from	-ate	verbal suffix
in-, im-	in, into	-cule, -icule	little
non-	not	-esce	to begin
ob-	toward, against	-(i)fy, -(e)fy	to make
per-	through, wrongly	-ible	able to be (cf. -able)
retro-	backward, behind	-it(e)	possessing
ultra-	beyond, exceedingly	-ory, -orium	place for

Prefix (Greek)	Meaning	Suffix (Greek)	Meaning/function
a-, an-	not, without	-archy	rule by
amphi-	both, around	-arium	little
ana-, an-	up, back, again	-cracy	rule by
cata-, cat-	down, against, very	-ectomy	surgical removal of
ec-	out, out of	-emia	condition of the blood
ecto-	outside, external	-graph	writing
eu-	good	-hedron	solid figure
hyper-	over, excessive	-itis	inflammation of
hypo-, hyp-	below	-maniac	one having madness
para-, par-	beside, disordered	-meter	measure
peri-	around, near	-oma	tumour
syn-, sym-	with, together	-tomy	surgical operation on

Action

Knowledge of the meanings of common Greek and Latin prefixes, suffixes and bases can be extremely useful in developing spelling and for understanding complex vocabulary in reading. An excellent book covering the theory behind word-building from Greek and Latin elements is:

> Ayers, D. M. (1986) *English Words from Latin and Greek Elements* (second edition). University of Arizona Press.

Meanings of prefixes and suffixes can be found in good dictionaries.

Task B2 – Semantic relations

Answers

Homonym

1(f) *Shells* has two meanings: weapon and sea creature.

Co-hyponyms

2(d) *Mallards*, *Canada geese* and *swans* are co-members of a set of inland water birds. They are hyponyms.

Synonym

3(a) *Abode* and *home* are used synonymously here. You may also have suggested that *home* and *work* are antonyms. This is correct, but sentence 4 was used to exemplify this relationship.

Antonym

4(b) *Hot* and *cold*, *favoured* and *opposed*, are antonyms.

Hyponym

5(c) The relationship between *food* and the words *salads*, *fish*, *bread*, *pickles and dips* is one of hyponymy.

Homonym

6(e) 'Green' is ambiguous and an example of a homonym.

Feedback

1(f) **Shells** *cascaded from the skies, landing not far from the soldiers as they marched along the shore,* **shells** *and pebbles crunching beneath their boots.*

The close proximity of these homonyms emphasizes the distinction of natural versus unnatural made between them. The semantic opposition of above and below, with the military shells coming from the skies and the natural shells being on the ground, is also emphasized.

2(d)   *Mallards, Canada geese and swans swam on the river, heedless of the boaters.*

5(c)   *There was an amazing array of food: salads, fish, freshly baked bread, pickles and dips.*

Co-hyponym
Co-ordinate
Superordinate

The birds in 2(d) and the foods in 5(c) form sets of the same type: inland water birds and food. In this way the birds are co-hyponyms or co-ordinates of the set of inland water birds. If the phrase *inland water birds* had been used, this would be a superordinate. In 5(c) *food* is in a relationship of hyponymy to *salads, fish,* etc. In these sentences, the co-hyponyms are found together, but over larger stretches of text co-hyponyms create cohesion. For example, in a recipe, ingredients, utensils and cooking methods are the three main lexical sets that one would expect to find. The members of each of these sets would be co-hyponyms:

eggs, flour, sugar, milk	(ingredients)
spoon, bowl, food processor	(utensils)
sieve, mix, beat, blend	(cooking methods)

> The word *ingredients* is a hyponym in relation to *eggs*.

Synonym

3(a)   *Her abode was conveniently situated near her work, but it is at home that we now find our heroine.*

Here the synonyms *abode* and *home* are used, although *home* is also used in contrast to *work*, so you may have said these are antonyms.

> Synonyms and antonyms are often used cohesively and to avoid repetition. See the feedback to Tasks C4 and D1 for more information.

4(b)   *She blew hot and cold; one day she favoured change and the next she opposed it.*

Antonym

Two relationships of antonymy are contained within this sentence. One of the most famous openings in literature uses antonyms: Dickens's *A Tale of Two Cities* begins 'It was the best of times, it was the worst of times ...'. The antonyms are accentuated by the grammatical parallelism of the phrases. That is, the phrases are grammatically identical. It is merely the relationships between the pairs of superlative adjectives and verbs that are different. This can also be described as antithesis in literary terminology.

Grammatical parallelism

Antithesis

Ambiguity

6(e)   *Our friend on the back benches is 'green', in several senses of the word.*

'Green' has a number of possible meanings, several of which could apply here: green meaning envious, youthful, environmentally aware, ill. We need preceding, or following, text or a link to a real event to give this statement a context to disambiguate the meaning, although in this case the usage is intentionally polysemantic and ambiguous.

> Look at Dylan Thomas's use of the word *green* in 'Fern Hill'.

Polysemantic

Action

Look at the way advertisements, poets and novelists use synonyms, antonyms and hyponymy for effect.

Task B3 – Semantics and variation

Answers

(a) *gee-gee* – The likely speaker is a very young child, since this word is characteristic of babies in their second year. However, adults do use the word when talking to young children and sometimes in the company of other adults, where it is marked for informality and possibly social class. This word is therefore restricted in its use in terms of age of speaker, social class, and informality.

trusty steed – The factors determining the use of this combination are likely to be literary. The semantic component of dependability in *steed* exists even without the adjective *trusty*, which makes the choice of this word motivated by a positive purpose such as in the plot of a story. Heroes and heroines use *steeds* to ride to the rescue, or to carry out some important task. The word is therefore restricted to literary or mock-literary genres.

equine colic – The likely user of this term is someone concerned with the medical condition of horses, such as a vet, stable keeper or horse owner. It is a formal usage. It is generically restricted to veterinary medicine and to users in this respect. Its use by a speaker in an informal setting would mark that speaker to others as a member of a particular speech community, such as a vet or a horse owner.

(b) 1. *residence*; 2. *abode*; 3. *pad*; 4. *gaff*; 5. *habitat*; 6. *property*; 7. *dwelling*

Feedback
Word choice is influenced by a complex set of social, generic and linguistic factors. Some words have neutral meanings and others are highly restricted to particular social or generic contexts.

The word *home*, for example, is a core vocabulary item used to refer to the place where we live. It is common to all language varieties and can be used in formal and informal settings. It is found early in the language of children. Its main restriction is that it has a wide neutral meaning. For example, it does not allow for the precise technical effect of *habitat* in scientific writing, or the aesthetic effect of *abode* in certain literary settings, and the precision or inclusivity of *property* in legal and pseudo legal texts, such as estate agents' particulars. In addition, it is not expected in some restricted collocations such as *governor's residence*, *humble abode* or *bachelor pad*.

In the examples, word choice is affected by collocation (1, 2, 3), dialect and informal spoken mode (4), genre or text type (5 and 6) and communicative purpose (7).

This exercise is aimed at raising your awareness of how a particular word choice affects the intended, implied or received meaning of a sentence. The inter-relationship of meaning and word choice is something to consider when speaking, writing and responding to reading. When speaking, word choice is affected by the formality and purpose of the occasion and the audience. For example, a headteacher's address to the school in assembly may contain some words that are selected from youth vernacular in order to demonstrate convergence with the audience. On the other hand, a reprimand of a single pupil in a one-to-one setting, in the headteacher's study, may take on a degree of formality by excluding this vocabulary in order to create formality and detachment.

Lexical restriction

Word choice

Core and specialized vocabulary

Convergence and detachment

Collins COBUILD English Dictionary defines *steed* as, 'a large strong horse used for riding; a literary word'.

During Key Stage 3 we should be moving pupils away from core vocabulary and aiming for extension and use of specialized and technical vocabulary where appropriate.

Think about the difference between the language you use to talk about the same subject to two people of different ages, gender or closeness.

When writing, word choice is also important. We learn that colloquialisms and idiomatic usage, such as *a lot*, *get the hang of* and *cracked jokes*, although acceptable in many speech settings, are usually avoided in writing. In addition, words such as *nice* and *good* should not be overused, and more appropriate descriptive and evaluative terms should be chosen. However, in the search for variety, simplicity of expression should not be abandoned in favour of complexity.

When reading and responding to text, we need to consider the effects created by particular word choices. Poets, novelists, advertising copywriters and journalists consider word choice carefully. As readers and teachers of reading, we need to be able to help pupils focus on word choice, intended meaning and effect. For example, in the media a recent television advert for bottled lager uses the word *cool*, playing on both its senses, including the popular slang usage, and pointing out that the beer is both iced and desirable. An example from literature, such as the second paragraph of the opening to John Fowles's *The French Lieutenant's Woman*, shows us that when the Cobb in Lyme Regis is described as 'a tiny Piraeus to a microscopic Athens', Fowles is carefully preparing the reader for other Hellenic allusions that are important to the development of the plot and the characters of Charles and Sarah.

Action
Examine a variety of texts, both spoken and written, from literature, non-fiction and the media, concentrating on lexical choice and variety. Collect samples of language that you could use with pupils to illustrate the ideas contained in this task and raise their awareness of the factors involved in word choice across genres and settings.

Task B4 – Phonemes and graphemes
Answers

(a) *ca<u>ts</u>*. An unvoiced consonant is a consonant that is produced without the vocal cords vibrating.

(b) *witt<u>y</u>*. Vowel graphemes are the six letters of the alphabet: a, e, i, o, u, y. 'Y' can be both a vowel and a consonant. In *witty* it is used as a vowel; in *yacht* it is used as a consonant.

(c) /ɔɪ/ in *v<u>oi</u>ce*. A diphthong is a complex vowel sound that is made by two vowel sounds blended together. Although you can feel and hear the movement between the two sounds in the /ɔɪ/ of *voice*, a diphthong is considered a single phoneme.

(d) /ʌ/ in *c<u>u</u>p*. A short vowel phoneme such as this can be distinguished from long vowel sounds, as in *w<u>ee</u>p*.

(e) *w<u>ee</u>p*. A vowel digraph is the term we use to describe two letters that are used in writing to make a single vowel sound. Sometimes they are double letters, as in *weep*, and sometimes they are two different letters as in *weak*.

(f) *ni<u>gh</u>t*. A consonant trigraph is the term we use to describe three letters that are used in writing to make a single consonant sound. Consonant trigraphs are not very numerous.

(g) *<u>w</u>rite*. Silent consonants are quite frequently found at the beginning of words, as in this example, and also within and at the ends of words, e.g. *lis<u>t</u>en; colum<u>n</u>*.

Glossary margin terms:
- Colloquialism
- Word choice and effect
- Allusion
- Unvoiced
- Vowel grapheme
- Diphthong
- Short vowel
- Digraph
- Trigraph
- Silent letter

Side notes:
Pupils beginning to react to the word choice implications of the written mode can produce over-ornate text that parodies well-written English, rather than successfully moving from speech to writing.

Dictionaries give important information about usage and restriction.

You can feel whether they are vibrating by holding the spot just below your Adam's apple.

Digraphs, trigraphs and silent letters complicate spelling. See the phonology section in Chapter 3.

(h) *dogs*. Voiced consonants involve sounds made by the vibration of the vocal cords.

Feedback
The terms used here represent only a sample of the terms used to describe the grapho-phonic system.

An understanding of the sound-to-letter correspondences in English is particularly important in the development of spelling. For example, digraphs and trigraphs present particular problems for weak spellers and test even the most able. *Manoeuvre* and *liaison*, for example, would be challenging to many adults. *Manoeuvre*, borrowed from the French, is difficult because of the vowel trigraph *oeu* to make the sound /uː/. *Liaison*, on the other hand, blends two vowel sounds, the second a diphthong /iː/, and /eɪ/, using three letters: *iai*.

The National Literacy Strategy (DfEE 1998) focuses work on phonics and spelling, and pupils who have followed schemes of work that develop these skills in the primary school will have studied the spelling of more complex words. However, much reinforcement and continued development is required as pupils pass through Key Stages 3 and 4, particularly with pupils with a diagnosis of dyslexia and weak spelling.

In addition, attention to other grapho-phonic aspects of words, such as common letter strings, blends, homophones, homographs and heteronyms, needs to be focused on.

Action
Examine the National Literacy Strategy to look for areas for reinforcement and development, particularly for weaker spellers and dyslexic pupils. Seek out advice on helping pupils with dyslexia from web sites and the Dyslexia Association.

> The term schwa is found and explained in the feedback to Task A.

> See Chapter 3 of *English for Primary Teachers* (in the Letts QTS Series) by Wray and Medwell (1997).

> Look up the British Dyslexia Association website on the Internet.

Margin terms: Voiced · Sound-to-letter correspondence · National Literacy Strategy · Dyslexia · Phonemic segmentation

....

Task B5 – Phonemic and syllabic segmentation
Answers
(a) The number of phonemes is given for each word and the structure of vowel and consonant sounds is shown as CVC, along with the phonetic transcription.

	WORD	PHONEMIC SEGMENTATION – No. of PHONEMES	VOWELS AND CONSONANTS	IPA TRANSCRIPTION
a	th/ou/ght	3	CVC	/θɔːt/
b	e/n/e/m/y	5	VCVCV	/enəmiː/
c	e/l/e/c/t	5	VCVCC	/elekt/
d	w/a/sh/i/ng	5 (or 6, if the 'g' is pronounced, as it is in some dialects)	CVCVC(C)	/wɒʃɪŋ/ or /wɒʃɪŋg/
e	s/ee	2	CV	/siː/
f	r/u/nn/er	4 (or 5 in accents that roll the 'r')	CVCV(C)	/rʌnə/ or /rʌnər/

(b) Syllables are shown in the table on page 44.

Syllabic segmentation

SYLLABIC SEGMENTATION				
	WORD	**NO. OF SYLLABLES**	**SEGMENTS**	**STRESSED SYLLABLE**
g	*elephant*	3	*el-e-phant*	first
h	*unselfish*	3	*un-sel-fish*	second
i	*notes*	1	*notes*	
j	*chocolate*	2	*cho-c(o)late*	first
k	*Worcester*	2	*Wor-c(es)ter*	first
l	*ridiculous*	4	*ri-dic-u-lous*	second

Feedback

Knowledge of phonemic and syllabic segmentation is important in the development of spelling. You need to be aware of the variety of graphic representations of single phonemes and the regularities and irregularities of the grapho-phonic system. Using the phonetic transcription of *thought* in the table on page 43, it is easy to see why the spelling of this word is so difficult: three sounds are represented by seven letters. Vowel and consonant digraphs (*th, ou, ee, sh, ng*) and trigraphs (*ght*) are the cause of these difficulties. Secondly, the presence of the schwa sound /ə/ in *enemy* and *runner* (and many spoken words) makes spelling problematic if writers rely on phonic knowledge. In addition, the unsounded final consonants (*washing* and *runner*) in many accents of English contribute to phonic spelling difficulty.

Schwa

Grapho-phonic system

Making matters more complicated, phoneme-to-grapheme correspondence is not one to one. For example, a single phoneme can be represented by a number of different combinations of graphemes.

Look at the table on page 98, which shows phoneme-to-grapheme correspondence.

e.g.   the sound /r/ in: *rug, horror, rhinoceros, write.*

And as there are at least 44 phonemes and only 26 graphemes to represent them, single graphemes represent several sounds. In the case of vowels, there are around 20 vowel sounds including diphthongs, and only six letters to represent them.

e.g.   the letter 'a' makes at least eight sounds: *mating, matting, marring, Mary, mall, majestic, many, manage.*

(PAYNE 1995)

Doubling
Silent letters

Double letters and silent vowels and consonants also complicate the spelling system. The grapho-phonic system is therefore inconsistent, although there is clearly sufficient consistency to prevent spelling being an impossibly difficult task. There are many consistent letter strings: *-ait, -all, -age, -ear, -ere, -eer, -eet, -ish, -ill ,-ost, -ole*, and *thr-, pr-, chr-, str-*, and so on. These, and the prefixes, suffixes and bases, help to provide some consistency of spelling.

Consistent letter strings

Knowledge of spelling rules can also improve spelling.

If we consider syllabification, looking at the table above we can see that the way words are spoken causes difficulty for spellers. Firstly, unstressed syllables are sometimes omitted altogether in speech:

> *chocolate* is pronounced /tʃɒklət/ and
> *Worcester* is pronounced /wʊstə/

Secondly, unstressed syllables present difficulties because of the indistinct, omitted or weak sounds.

The vowel sound in each of these words is the weak schwa sound /ə/.

> *elephant*   *chocolate*   *Worcester*   *ridiculous*

Action
Making efforts to understand pupils' spelling difficulties and improving your own will entail some understanding of grapho-phonic relationships and syllabification. There is some evidence that spelling is developmental, moving from phonetic guesses and knowledge of letter strings and sequences to correct spelling. As pupils move towards correct spelling, there will be some interference from the sounds of spoken words and some phonetic guessing of unfamiliar and new words, but pupils need to move away from reliance on phonetic guessing in order to become correct spellers. There are a number of useful books that will help you develop knowledge and pedagogy:

Gentry, G. R. (1981) 'Developmental Spelling' in *Reading Teacher*, Vol. 34, No. 4.

Montgomery, D. (1997) *Spelling: Remedial Strategies*. Cassell.

Payne, J. (1995) *Collins COBUILD English Guides 8: Spelling*. HarperCollins.

Snowling, M. J. (ed.) (1993) *Children's Written Language Difficulties: Assessment and Management*. Routledge.

Torbe, M. (1978) *Teaching Spelling*. Ward Lock

Task B6 – Phonology and poetic effect

Answers
Phonological features:

Phonological features of poetry

alliteration	*hue of health* (line 148); *on syren shores, the salt sea-spry* (l. 157) and many other examples.
assonance	Repetition of a range of vowel sounds occurs in each stanza: /aɪ/ *why, white, thy; hue, dewy* (stanza 1); /ʌst/ *dost, lustrous; why, eye, light, night, syren, spry* (stanza 2) /ɪ/ *ditties, give, nightingale, listen* (stanza 3)
consonance	The consonant sound /st/ is repeated throughout: *midmost forest* (l. 144) *dost* (second line of each stanza) *is't* (l. 151) *lustrous* (l. 154) *mayst* (l. 163) *constant* (ll. 178 and 181)
couplet	Couplets feature strongly in this poem, with two couplets in each of stanzas 1 to 3 and three in stanzas 4 and 5.
euphony/ dissonance	'Sweetness of sound' is created through the use of assonance, the use of couplets and the rhymes, particularly those with long vowel sounds. However, the effect is not completely euphonic, the consonance and alliteration of harsh consonants contributing to a persistent note of dissonance.
feminine rhyme	Bi-syllabic rhymes are found throughout: *sorrow* and *borrow* feature in each stanza; *flower* and *bower* (stanza 4); *sorrow* and *morrow* (stanza 5); *cheerly* and *dearly* (stanza 5).

> Many features could have been listed. You may have commented on a greater number than those listed here.

> The stanzas referred to here are the stanzas of the roundelay following the three lines introducing it.

	In addition to these words of two syllables, there are a number of rhymes involving two syllables across words: *evening pale* and *nightingale* (stanza 3); *so kind* (twice); *deceive her* and *leave her* (stanza 5)
homophone	The word *mourning* (l. 160) is used in close association with *evening* (l. 161), bringing to mind its homophone *morning*. In this way the poet plays on the meanings of both words, even though the homophone is not used here.
intonation	Rising intonation is a pervasive feature of this extract, in the continued use of questions.
masculine rhyme	The majority of the rhymes are masculine, rhyming with one syllable.
refrain	Repeated phrases and lines are used in this extract, chiefly at the beginning of stanzas (*Oh Sorrow,/Why dost borrow*), with variation in the final stanza and additional repetition in lines 178 and 181.
repetition	Words and lines are repeated in the use of refrain.
roundelay	Described in Cuddon's (1992) *The Penguin Dictionary of Literary Terms and Literary Theory* as 'a short simple song with a refrain ... where refrain and repetition are used extensively.'
sight rhyme	The sight rhyme in *blushes/bushes* (ll. 149 and 150) would otherwise produce a feminine rhyme with both syllables rhyming.
sound/letter	As one reads, one is aware of the play on sound and letter differences: in the sight rhyme of *blushes* and *bushes* (ll. 149 and 150), the written but not spoken repetition of *st* in *mayst listen* (l. 163) and the alliteration /k/ in *constant* and *kind* (stanza 6).

Many of the phonological features have a unifying effect in this short roundelay in Keats's 'Endymion'. Long vowel sounds reinforce the mournful, pitying tone, with the dissonant, harsh and repeated consonants contributing to its petulance and bitterness. The rising intonation of the many questions continues this mournful note, seemingly resolved in the final stanza, where the interrogative mood is replaced by a declarative, but is then reprised with a final sigh in the last line.

Feedback

This exercise asks you to perform a task that isolates a large number of phonological effects in a single poem. This is done for the purpose of this audit and it is not suggested that you approach the teaching of poetry in such a way. It is more important to be able to teach pupils to appreciate the effects of poetry and respond to them. This will entail appreciation of the phonological (and lexical and grammatical) resources used by the poet, but these should emerge in writing about and discussion of the poem rather than as skills to be learnt in isolation, although careful selection of texts and extracts will enable you to target particular features of phonology.

Knowledge of key terminology is important to us as teachers, equipping us to talk about these effects and to teach pupils to talk and write using technical vocabulary to describe features they wish to comment on.

Sidebar (left margin):

Interrogative

Declarative

Phonological effect

Appreciation and response

Sidebar (right):

Technical terms should be introduced when they arise from a particular poem being read, rather than as a focus for study in themselves.

Action

A particularly useful work of reference is:

> Cuddon, J. A. (1992) *The Penguin Dictionary of Literary Terms and Literary Theory* (third edition). Penguin.

Use it in association with the poetry you read to gain a fuller understanding of the language of phonology in relation to its effect in poetry. It is also a useful reference source of poetic forms. Another informative book is:

> Leech, G. (1969) *A Linguistic Guide to English Poetry*. Longman.

For poetic forms, see the feedback on Task D2.

Section C:

The grammatical system of spoken and written language

Task C1 – Word class

Answers

(a)   Stanza 1: The table below shows suggestions for replacements to the eleven words in stanza 1. These suggestions have been made by students who have done this exercise.

	WORD CLASS(ES)	EXAMPLES GIVEN BY STUDENTS				
brillig	adjective	*stormy*	*bright*	*windy*	*stormy*	*thunderous*
slithy	adjective	*shiny*	*slender*	*slimy*	*frothy*	*shiny*
tove	noun	*trees*	*trees*	*branches*	*waves*	*boats*
gyre	verb	*sparkle*	*bend*	*jump*	*crash*	*pitch*
gimble	verb	*creak*	*sway*	*groan*	*thunder*	*roll*
wabe	noun	*wind*	*night*	*night*	*bay*	*waves*
mimsy	adjective	*misty*	*alive*	*funky*	*frightened*	*seasick*
borogoves	noun	*valleys*	*clouds*	*newts*	*fishes*	*sailors*
mome	noun	*moon's*	*moon*	*frogs*	*moon*	*buckets*
raths	noun or verb	*rays*	*shone*	*raved*	*shone*	*were*
outgrabe	verb, adv. or adj.	*shone*	*gently*	*on*	*down*	*full*

> Stanza 2: *frumious* could be replaced by any negative adjective (as *the Bandersnatch* is shunned); *-ious* is an adjectival suffix suggesting this.

> Stanza 3: *vorpal* could be replaced by any adjective that complements *sword*. *Manxome* could be replaced by another negative adjective. *-al*, *-some* and *-som* are adjectival suffixes.

> Stanza 4: *uffish* and *tulgey* could be replaced by adjectives, *-ish* and *-y* being adjectival suffixes. *Whiffling* and *burbled* should be replaced with verbs, preserving the temporal inflections.

(b)   noun – *sword, hand, time, foe, Tumtum tree, thought*
adjective – *vorpal, long, manxome*
main verb – *took, sought, rested, stood*
auxiliary verb – *did* (stanza 1)

adverb – *awhile*
pronoun – *He* (× 3)
preposition – *in* (× 2), *by*
conjunction – *So, and*
determiner – *his, the* (× 2)
possessive adjective – *his*

Feedback

(a) This exercise is intended to demonstrate that knowledge of word class and word order is securely in place, though often at a subconscious level. Students who do this exercise never fail to produce a highly consistent set of word-class choices. We can see from the table that in the majority of cases only one word-class choice is possible. Knowledge of word order tells us that adjectives are most commonly found before nouns and after the verb 'to be', adverbs come after verbs and before adjectives, and verbs follow nouns or subjects.

The most problematic words to replace were probably *mome, raths* and *outgrabe*. You can see from the table that three word-class combinations are possible and were suggested by the students:

noun, verb, adverb: *moon shone down*
noun, verb, adjective: *buckets were full*
noun, noun, verb: *moon's rays shone*

The noun, verb, adverb combination is the one most commonly chosen by this sample of students.

Your sub-conscious or conscious knowledge of English word classes and their positions and functions in sentences is reinforced by knowledge of common suffixes. Suffixes help us identify word class and can be used to create nonce words and neologisms, such as the ones created by Lewis Carroll. The suffix *-ig* on the word *brillig* is an Anglo-Saxon adjectival suffix, equivalent to *-y* in modern English, and coincidentally many of the students chose adjectives with this suffix.

(b) In the second exercise, the abstract noun *thought* may have been incorrectly classified as a verb. Nouns commonly follow prepositions, although often with a determiner or article, as in *by the Tumtum tree*. Another difficulty may have arisen in distinguishing between the pronoun *he* and the possessive adjective (or determiner) *his*. Pronouns indicate that a noun phrase could be substituted, whereas possessive adjectives and determiners are used at the beginning of a noun phrase. 'The blacksmith's son' would fit the pronoun *he* in this stanza, but *his* could not be replaced with a noun phrase. *His* has been described as both a possessive adjective and a determiner. This is because grammars describe this class of words in both these ways. The first is more precise.

Finally, the adverb *awhile* may have been difficult to identify, not having the common *-ly* adverbial suffix. Adverbs are problematic from this point of view. There are many less easily identifiable ones, such as *now, then, nevertheless, however*. Many of these can be confused with conjunctions, because of their conjunctive usage.

Sidebar labels: Word class · Function · Nonce words and neologisms · Abstract noun · Pronoun · Possessive adjective · Adverb · Conjunction

Humpty Dumpty explains the meanings of the nonsense words to Alice in Chapter 7 of *Through the Looking Glass*.

An effective way of identifying word class is to learn an archetype or memorable word for each one. For example, *in* is a preposition; *happy* is an adjective. You can then try replacing a word you want to test with the archetype to see whether the archetype performs the same function in the same setting. Word class means that all words in a class can do just that, although in the case of adverbs, as described above, this is not quite so straightforward.

Archetype

Action
Other authors, such as Roald Dahl, James Joyce, Edward Lear, Spike Milligan and P. G. Wodehouse, create neologisms and portmanteau words in similar ways, often for humorous effect. Advertising copywriters also use word coining for novel effect. Looking at words created in this way, and alerting pupils to the resources for creating new words, can raise awareness of word-forming suffixes, increase knowledge of word class, and be fun.

Portmanteau words

Word coining

> Remember that you can always use a dictionary to identify word class, if in doubt.

A useful reference book is:
> Crystal, D. (1996) *Rediscover Grammar* (second edition). Longman.

Task C2 – Word function

Answers

Modal auxiliary

(a)   Modal auxiliary – e.g. *She will be arriving home at six o'clock.* Auxiliary verbs come before verbs in verb phrases. In this example, *will* and *be* are auxiliaries and *arriving* is the main verb. The verb phrase is *will be arriving*. Modal auxiliaries are words such as *will*, *must*, *can* and *may* that give us information about intention, necessity, possibility or probability.

> See also answers to Task A on page 35.

Adverb

(b)   Adverb – see answer to Task A on page 34.

Intransitive verb

(c)   Intransitive verb – e.g. *The dog slept beside the fire.* Intransitive verbs do not have objects. In the example, *beside the fire* is not an object. It is an adjunct of place, giving information about <u>where</u> the dog slept, rather than <u>what</u> it slept. The verb 'to sleep' is almost always used intransitively, although in the sentence *She slept the sleep of the righteous* it is used transitively. Here, *the sleep of the righteous* is the object, denoting <u>what</u> is slept.

> Intransitive verbs cannot be made passive.

Co-ordinating conjunction

(d)   Co-ordinating conjunction – e.g. *We thought we were doing well but we were mistaken.* Co-ordinating conjunctions are words such as *and*, *but* and *or*. They join words in pairs and lists (*now and then*; *fat, friendly and feline*) and free clauses to make compound sentences, as in the example.

> See pages 56–57 for more on compound sentences.

Superlative adjective

(e)   Superlative adjective – e.g. *The greatest favour you could do me would be to give me a lift to the station.* Superlative adjectives are formed by adding the *-est* suffix to adjectives. However, generally adjectives with more than two syllables cannot be formed in this way. Their comparative and superlative forms are made using *more* and *most*, e.g. *most beautiful*. Adjectives come before nouns and after the verb 'to be' in English. A common mistake in children's speech and writing is to use both ways of forming comparatives at the same time, e.g. *I thought the exam would be more easier.*

Comparative adjective

Proper noun

(f)   Proper noun – e.g. <u>*Christmas Day*</u> *falls on a* <u>*Saturday*</u> *this year.*
       Proper nouns are names of people, places and events and are
       always capitalized. They function in the same way as other
       nouns, being found as the subject and object of sentences and
       after prepositions in prepositional phrases.

Feedback

If you have not studied grammar during your degree, or at A level, you
may be restricted to talking about adjectives as describing words and
verbs as actions. This is clearly below the level at which you need to
operate professionally. The word classes chosen for this exercise are
merely a sample, but from your response to the task you should have a
good idea about how your level of knowledge matches what is needed.
Word classes are merely labels for classifications of words with similar
functions. In order to develop your knowledge follow the action below.

Action

The glossary of any good book on grammar will provide clear
explanations and examples of all word classes. Crystal's (1996)
introduction is recommended (see page 49) and other more detailed
books on grammar that deal with word class are:

> Quirk, R., Greenbaum. S., Leech, G. N. and Svartvik, J. A. (1985)
> *A Comprehensive Grammar of the English Language*. Longman.

> Sinclair, J. (ed.) (1990) *Collins COBUILD English Grammar*.
> Collins ELT.

Task C3 – Word order

Answers

(a)   *To give at evening pale/Unto the nightingale,/That thou mayst listen
       the cold dews among* can be rewritten as: *To give at* <u>*pale*</u> *evening unto
       the nightingale, that thou mayst listen* <u>*among*</u> *the cold dews.*
       In the example, the adjective *pale* is found after (rather than
       before) the noun *evening* in order to make it rhyme with
       nightingale. This word order is allowed in poetry. The
       preposition *among* is found at the end of the prepositional phrase
       the cold dews among, rather than at the beginning. Again this word
       order is found in poetry, in this case making the rhyme with
       tongue, found earlier.

(b)   *All mimsy were the borogoves* can be rewritten as: *The borogoves
       were* <u>*all mimsy*</u>.
       In the example, the subject of the clause *the borogoves* is found
       after the verb, and the complement, *all mimsy*, is in initial
       position. This is a reversal of the usual order of clause elements.
       Reversal of clause elements here is motivated by the rhyme
       scheme, as *borogoves* rhymes with *the slithy toves* of the first line of
       'Jabberwocky'.

Reversal

(c)   *Long time the manxome foe he sought – /So rested he by the Tumtum
       tree,* can be rewritten as: <u>*He sought*</u> *the manxome foe [*<u>*for*</u>*] a long time
       – So* <u>*he*</u> *rested by the Tumtum tree.*
       In the example, there are several marked changes of word order.

Foregrounding

Internal rhyme

Firstly, the adjunct of time, *long time*, although shortened, is foregrounded by being in initial position. This gives greater emphasis to the duration of time than if placed at the end of the clause. Secondly, the subject of the sentence, *he*, and the verb, *sought*, come after the object, *the manxome foe*. This is again motivated by rhyme, as *sought*, and not *foe*, is the word that is rhymed. Finally, in the second clause the subject is again found after the verb, this time for the purposes of internal rhyme. When the position of subject and verb are reversed, the subject *he* comes on the stressed beat of a foot, half way through the line, and thus forms an internal rhyme with *tree*.

Active and passive

(d) Active – *The clock* is the actor and *stopped* is the action.

(e) Active – *William* is the actor; *the television* is what is switched on.

(f) Passive – The actor or agent is *the policeman;* the affected thing is *the traffic*. Since the actor is in object position and the affected is in subject position, this sentence is passive. The presence of the verb 'to be' (*been*) as an auxiliary in the verb phrase and the preposition *by* also indicate a passive. The active sentence would be: *The policeman had stopped the traffic.*

> The subject in sentences (f) and (i) is passive. It is not doing anything; something is done to it.

(g) Active – *The vicar* is the actor and *the service* is what had begun.

(h) Active – *The ducks* are the actors and *swimming* is the action. Since *swimming* is used intransitively, there is no object; *on the lake* is where they are swimming (an adjunct).

(i) Passive – This is an agentless passive, since we only know what was broken, not who or what did the breaking: *the grandchildren* or *laughter*, for example.

(j) Active – See the feedback below for an explanation of this sentence and the difference between it and sentence (i).

(k) Active – This is the active form of sentence (f), although there is a difference in tense.

Feedback

Passive transformation

The transformation of passive sentences from active sentences is governed by a few simple rules. Let us look at the transformation of two active sentences. In both sentences the subject is *the dog* and the object *the bone*:

The dog is eating the bone.	Active verb (progressive *-ing* form)
The dog ate the bone.	Active verb (past tense).

Reversal of subject and object

Step 1. The position of subject and object are reversed, so that the object becomes subject and the subject becomes agent. The preposition *by* is added to the agent:

The bone	*is being eaten*	*by the dog.*
The bone	*was eaten*	*by the dog.*

Omission of agent

The agent may be omitted in a passive sentence, making it agentless.

The bone was eaten.

Agentless passives are used when the agent is unknown, immediately recoverable from previous text, or when the writer wants to create ambiguity or hide the agent.

Addition of auxiliary and past participle

Step 2. The verb phrase changes: the verb 'to be' is used to create an auxiliary whose tense has to be matched to the main verb and the main verb is changed to the past participle.

> *is eat**ing***   (main verb – present progressive)
> *is be**ing** eaten*   (auxiliary takes the progressive; main verb changes to the past participle)
> ***ate***   (main verb – past tense)
> ***was** eaten*   (auxiliary takes the past tense; main verb changes to the past participle)

Where there is an auxiliary verb already, as in *is eating*, the auxiliary forming the passive is placed between it (or them, where there is more than one auxiliary in the verb phrase) and the main verb.

Using this knowledge, we can now distinguish active from passive. Sentences (h), (i) and (j) in the task look grammatically identical:

> (h) *The ducks were swimming on the lake.*
> (i) *The silence was broken,*
> (j) *The children were happy.*

However, (h) and (j) are active and (i) is passive. This is because the verb 'to be' is used in a different form in the verb phrase of each sentence. The verb phrase is highlighted in bold:

> (h) *The ducks **were swimming** on the lake.*
> (i) *The silence **was broken**,*
> (j) *The children **were** happy.*

The verb 'to be'

Firstly, we can say that in (h) and (i) the verb 'to be' forms the auxiliary verbs *were* and *was*, coming before the main verbs *swimming* and *broken,* whereas in (j) the verb 'to be' is the main verb and *happy* is an adjective. The verbs 'to be' and 'to have' share this dual capability of being able to be both main verb and auxiliary verb before a main verb. One has to decide which function the verb is performing in a particular sentence – auxiliary or main verb.

Auxiliaries are not found alone. They always accompany a main verb, so *were* in (j) cannot be a main verb.

Transitive and intransitive

Secondly, the verb phrases in (h) and (i), although both consisting of an auxiliary and a main verb, are different: *swimming* is an intransitive verb with no object; *broken* is a transitive verb but used passively, so the object is in the subject position and it is agentless.

Knowledge of word order, including the use of the passive, is particularly useful when analysing the stylistic effects created in poetry, novels and non-fiction (particularly advertising text). It is also invaluable to the study of the history of language and of texts not in modern English, such as Chaucer and Shakespeare.

Action
A particularly useful book that examines grammar, vocabulary, phonology and style is:

> Freeborn, D. (1996) *Style*. Macmillan.

Many texts and examples are used and explained, making it particularly useful as a coursebook for pupils at A level and a suitable text for self-study following this audit.

Task C4 – Cohesion within sentences

Answers

The two extracts are shown below, labelled according to the following key to show the variety of cohesive devices.

KEY

reference: [ ] **bold**   ellipsis: *[missing words]*
↑

lexical cohesion: <u>underline</u>   conjunction: *italics*

(a)   The time now approached for [Lady Russell's] return ↑ *[to Kellynch]*; the day was even
  [for Lady Russell's return]
  fixed ↑, and [Anne,] being engaged to join [her] as soon as [she] was

  <u>resettled</u>, was looking forward to [an early removal to Kellynch,] and
  [Anne was]
  ↑ beginning to think how [her] <u>own comfort</u> was likely to be affected by [it.]

(b)   [Lady Russell] had only to listen composedly, and wish [them] happy; *but*

  internally [her] <u>heart revelled in angry pleasure</u>, <u>in pleased contempt</u>, *that*

  a man who at twenty-three had seemed to understand somewhat of <u>the</u>

  <u>value of an Anne Elliot</u>, should eight years *afterwards*, be <u>charmed by a</u>

  <u>Louisa Musgrove</u>.

Feedback

The concept of cohesion comes from Halliday and Hasan (1976). Put simply, it is the process through which, at sentence level, we identify links between words in a sentence, or, at a textual level, the way sentences and paragraphs hang together. In this section we are focusing on the ties between words within a sentence. Halliday and Hasan identified five types of cohesive tie: reference, substitution, ellipsis, conjunction and lexical cohesion.

<u>Reference</u>

Reference is made through the use of personal and possessive pronouns and determiners:

PERSONAL PRONOUNS		POSSESSIVE PRONOUNS	POSSESSIVE DETERMINERS
SUBJECT	OBJECT	*mine, yours, his, hers, its, yours, theirs*	*my, your, his, her, its, your, their*
I, you, he, she, it, we, you, they	*me, you, him, her, it, you, them*		

Reference using these items is called personal reference.

Task D2 looks at textual cohesion.

Side labels:
Intra-sentential cohesion

Cohesive tie

Reference

Demonstrative reference

Halliday and Hasan also identify demonstrative reference, using the demonstratives *here, there, now, then, this, that, these* and *those*. These ties demonstrate proximity in time or space between the items they refer to.

Anaphoric and cataphoric reference

Reference can be anaphoric (pointing backwards) or cataphoric (pointing forwards). Backward-pointing reference is the most common; this is logical, as in the process of reading we build comprehension based on what we have read, although we also predict. Cohesive ties that link back to what we have read consolidate meaning, whereas ones that point forward involve us in some anticipation of what we are going to read.

In sentence (a) we can see four examples of anaphoric reference. This is where the pronouns (*her, she* and *it*) refer back to preceding items (*Lady Russell, Anne* and either *Lady Russell's return* or *an early removal to Kellynch*, or both). In the case of the cohesive item *it*, we should note that what it stands for is not merely a noun but a whole nominal group.

In sentence (b) there are two further examples, although the first refers to a previous sentence and so is not intra-sentential cohesion.

Ellipsis

Ellipsis

Ellipsis is the process of omitting words, phrases or clauses that are recoverable from an earlier part of the sentence (or text). Meaning is not lost but consolidated through this process.

In sentence (a) there are three instances of ellipsis, although the first is not intra-sentential but relates to an earlier sentence, so is textually cohesive. In each of the remaining cases, the ellipsed phrase is immediately recoverable from earlier in the sentence.

> For a fuller description of these categories, see Halliday and Hasan (1976).

Lexical cohesion

Lexical cohesion

In sentence (a) *Lady Russell's return, she was resettled* and *her own comfort* are all lexically linked. *Resettled* is reiterating and expanding on *return*, and *comfort* and *settled* are semantically linked. In addition *Lady Russell* and *her* [Anne's] *own* are compared and contrasted.

Sentence (b) is rich in lexical cohesion. There is some use of synonymy and antonymy: *happy* and *pleased; happy* and *angry* and *pleasure* and *contempt*. Grammatical parallelism and oxymoron contribute to the synonymy and antonymy of *in angry pleasure, in pleased contempt*. Similarly the parallelism and semantic opposition of *value of an Anne Elliot* and *charmed by a Louisa Musgrove* emphasize the differences between the two characters and make Louisa's charms negative attributes.

> Cohesion is an important aspect of reading and writing development. Its presence makes for well-constructed writing and reading rich in meaning, because of the relationships within and between sentences.

Conjunction

Conjunction

Halliday and Hasan describe four types of conjunction: additive, adversative, temporal and causal. Conjunctions are not the only word class that contribute to this kind of cohesion. Adverbial phrases and adverbs, such as *an hour later* or *next day,* contribute to the effect of sequence.

EXAMPLES OF COHESIVE CONJUNCTION			
ADDITIVE	**ADVERSATIVE**	**TEMPORAL**	**CAUSAL**
and, or, thus	*but, though, rather*	*an hour later, then*	*because, so, therefore*

Additive, adversative, temporal and causal conjunction

Sentence (b) is full of adversatives, emphasized firstly by the adversative conjunction *but,* and also by the antonymy within the parallelism described above. The phrases surrounding this conjunction tell us that the external demonstration of composure by Lady Russell and her internal emotion are in conflict. Internal and external oppositions and oppositions of characters are mirrored by the semantic relations in the sentence. These are all important resources for satirical writing that examines false values.

Action
The theory of cohesion is explained in:

> Halliday, M. A. K. and Hasan, R. (1976) *Cohesion in English.*
> Longman.

A useful book which applies Halliday and Hasan's theory to reading development is:

> Chapman, J. (1983) *Reading Development and Cohesion.*
> Heinemann Educational.

Task C5 – Complex sentences

Answers

Simple sentence

(a) One clause, therefore a simple sentence; *for the register* is a prepositional phrase, not a clause.

Subordinate and main clause

(b) Two clauses, the first subordinate and the second main, therefore a complex sentence.

When we got there,	subordinate clause, introduced by subordinating conjunction *when.*
we went into a room.	main clause

Complex sentence

(c) Two clauses, the first main and the second subordinate, therefore a complex sentence.

Mark was really excited	main clause
because they were going	subordinate clause, introduced by the
on a plane.	subordinating conjunction *because.*

(d) Complex sentence containing four clauses:

I twisted the rusty key in the lock;	main clause
it snapped against my skin	main clause
as I placed the rubber band	subordinate clause, introduced by subordinating conjunction *as*
which it was attached to	embedded relative clause
over my wrist.	remainder of subordinate clause

Compound sentence

(e) Compound sentence containing three main clauses, all co-ordinated by *and*.

We went inside school for the register	main clause
and	co-ordinating conjunction
the coach came	main clause
and	co-ordinating conjunction
we got on the coach.	main clause

(f) Simple sentence containing one clause.

Feedback

Syntax

The study of syntax involves the study of the grammatical units that make up sentences. We can see these units as a hierarchy, with sentence as the largest unit and morpheme as the smallest unit of grammatical meaning. After sentence come clause, phrase and word in descending order, with each sentence containing one or more clauses, each clause containing one or more phrases and each phrase containing one or more words. We have seen that words contain one or more morphemes. Sentence (b), used as an example, demonstrates this hierarchy:

Hierarchy of units:
Sentence

Clause

Phrase

Word

When we got there,	*we went into a room*	sentence
[When we got there,]	*[we went into a room.]*	two clauses
[we] [got] [there,]	*[we] [went] [into a room]*	three phrases in each clause
[When] [we] [got] [there,]	*[we] [went] [into | a | room]*	single word phrases and one three-word phrase

> Units move downwards from greater to lesser status and meaning.

This task examines sentence type, which is dependent on the number and type of clauses contained in the sentence. In order to identify clause type we need to understand the difference between clause and phrase. The simplest definition is that a clause must have a verb. This excludes phrases such as *into a room* and *through the clear glass* because there is no verb. Phrases can sometimes be incorrectly mistaken for clauses because of their length.

Imperative

It is a misconception that syntactic units are identified by length. Sentence and word, although superior and inferior in terms of their hierarchical status, can be identical in length. For example, a single word, *Stop!*, is also an imperative clause and a sentence. By contrast, a number of words, such as *through the glimmering glass* or *the cat with the amazing whiskers,* although longer than the sentence *Stop!*, are phrases (prepositional phrase and noun phrase) and therefore below sentence and clause in the hierarchy of syntactical units.

Sentence type

Once the number of clauses has been identified, their type needs to be looked at in order to be able to describe the sentence type.

- Simple sentences are 'simple' to identify because they contain single clauses, as in (a) and (f) in the task. They contain only main clauses and do not contain subordinate clauses, because these cannot stand alone.

- Multi-clause sentences are divided into two types: compound and complex. Compound sentences contain two or more main clauses linked by co-ordinating conjunctions or punctuation.

- Complex sentences contain clauses of two types: main and subordinate clauses.

Main clause

Main clauses are clauses that are able to stand alone. A good test for this is to see whether the unit could begin with a capital letter and end with a full stop. For example, in:

Mark was really excited because they were going on a plane.

the first clause can stand alone, but the second cannot:

Mark was really excited.   sentence
Because they were going
on a plane.   not a sentence; not a main clause

Subordinate clause

Subordinate clauses, therefore, cannot stand alone. They must always be joined or bound to a main clause:

main clause   subordinate clause
[*Mark was really excited*]   [*because they were going on a plane.*]

Co-ordinating and subordinating conjunctions

Main clauses are joined by co-ordinating conjunctions (*and, but, so, or*) or punctuation (comma and semi-colon), and subordinate clauses are introduced by subordinating conjunctions (*when, while, because, if, so that, in order to, although*) and often marked by punctuation. Here are sentences (b) to (e), with conjunctions marked by bold and clauses indicated by square brackets:

(b)   [**When** we got there,] [we went into a room.]
(c)   [Mark was really excited] [**because** they were going on a plane.]
(d)   [I twisted the rusty key in the lock] **and** [it snapped against my skin] [**as** I placed the rubber band [**which** it was attached to] over my wrist.]
(e)   [We went inside school for the register] **and** [the coach came] **and** [we got on the coach.]

We can now say why (b), (c) and (d) are complex sentences and why (e) is a compound sentence. In (e), all the clauses are joined by the conjunction *and*. In sentences (b) and (c), each of the subordinate clauses is joined to a main clause by subordinating conjunctions, the clause boundaries marked by commas. Sentence (d) has the two main clauses joined by *and* and the subordinate clause (with the further embedded subordinate clause within it) is introduced by the subordinating conjunction *as*. We could therefore describe sentence (d) as compound-complex.

Clause boundaries

Writing development

The extent to which pupils use co-ordination and subordination in their writing can be a measure of development. The programme of study (standard English and language study – writing; Key Stages 3 and 4) states: 'Pupils should be encouraged to broaden their understanding of the principles of sentence grammar ... phrase, clause and sentence structure – the use of complex grammatical structures ... ; the use of main and subordinate clauses and phrases.' In addition, the marking of end-of-key-stage tests and teacher assessment of levels of attainment look for use of complex sentences and a range of subordinate clauses.

Style

However, degree of subordination cannot always be used as a measure of development. It is also a matter of style. For instance, novelists use

---

Simple sentences always contain main clauses, although you will come across examples of subordinate (and non-finite) clauses presented as sentences in students' writing right up to adulthood. A good understanding of syntax and correct application of punctuation in writing are, therefore, strongly interrelated.

Co-ordinating conjunctions are not part of the clause, and are therefore placed outside the square brackets in (d) and (e) here, whereas subordinating conjunctions are part of the subordinate clause, so are within the square brackets indicating the subordinate clauses.

simple and complex sentences for different reasons. In his book, *Style*, Dennis Freeborn (1996) discusses the distribution and effect of simple sentences in George Orwell's *Animal Farm*. He notes that simple sentences are 'placed in strategic positions', which produces clarity of important messages, as in:

> **It was a savage, bitter battle.** *A cow, three sheep, and two geese were killed, and nearly everyone was wounded.* [My use of bold.]

He also notes the co-ordination and compound sentences that characterize Conrad's *Heart of Darkness*, representing a feature of speech appropriate to this spoken narrative.

Action

Examine samples of pupils' writing and marking criteria for Key Stage 3 writing tasks and analyse the effects and usage of simple, compound and complex sentences in pupils' writing and in fiction and non-fiction.

Task C6 – Co-ordination and subordination

Answers

(a)	noun phrase	(e)	noun phrase
(b)	verb phrase	(f)	adjectival phrase
(c)	prepositional phrase	(g)	subordinate clause; finite clause
(d)	relative clause; subordinate clause	(h)	main clause; finite clause

Phrase complexity

(i) <u>Complexity of phrase development</u>
When we look at the three texts, we can see that noun phrases become more complex, moving from single nouns such as *school*, *coach* and *milk* (Text 1), with no adjectival pre-modification and no post-modification in the form of prepositional phrases or defining relative clauses, to more complex noun phrases with adjectives, such as *a pretty normal boy* (Text 2), and post-modifying defining relative clauses – *the clanking that was coming from below me* (Text 3).

Noun phrase

TEXT	PRE-MODIFICATION	NOUN	POST-MODIFICATION
	DEVELOPING COMPLEXITY IN NOUN PHRASES		
1	*the* *the baby*	*school* *coach* *milk* *swans*	
2	*a pretty normal* *lots of* *the first* *a sudden little* *a beautiful white shiny*	*boy* *things* *day* *whirlpool* *palace*	
3	*the hotel* *my two best* *my brother's* *the* *the glimmering glass* *the cool clean* *the dark and damp* *the rubber* *the surprisingly dry*	*swimming pool* *friends* *screams* *clanking* *windows* *water* *locker* *band* *floor*	*that was coming from below me* *which it was attached to*

Cohesion

Noun phrases in Text 1 are repetitive, with no cohesive pronouns apart from the use of *we* to report the event, whereas the writers of Texts 2 and 3 are using personal and demonstrative pronouns (*This* – Text 3) cohesively to refer to preceding events, objects and people. (Post-modification of nouns appears only in Text 3.)

Adjectival use

Adjectival use develops from almost no use of adjectives (*good* is the only one used in Text 1) to use of lists and comparatives (*warmer* in Text 2) and alliterative adjectival use (*glimmering glass windows; cool clean water*) and sub-modified adjectives (*surprisingly dry floor*) in Text 3.

Prepositional phrase

Text 1 is rich in prepositional phrases (*into a room*), but these are used repetitively in a single position in the sentence, after the verb or object. In Text 3, the writer uses prepositional phrases for effect in clause initial position, such as in <u>*with a single shudder*</u> the lift doors opened.

Adverb

Adverbs are present in Texts 2 and 3 and are used emphatically in sentence initial position (*down* and *suddenly* – Text 2) and to sub-modify adjectives in Text 3. A sophisticated adverb, *swiftly*, is used by the writer of Text 3.

Verb phrase

Verb phrases are restricted in terms of length and lexical choice in Text 1, with *went* and *see/saw* accounting for a large number. The writer of Text 2 uses a greater variety of verbs, including the reporting verb *said*. There is some complexity, with the progressive *-ing* form used with the past tense. The writer of Text 3 has mastered the use of complex verb phrases, including modals (*could*) and expressing future action in the past: *This was going to be fun*. There is some use of phrasal verbs in *take advantage of* and *made my way*, increasing the variety of verbs and extending meaning beyond core items such as 'to go'. There are examples of other non-core verbs – *cascaded, entered, registered, placed, slapped* – that are used appropriately.

Extending meaning

Clause variety

(j)   <u>Variety of clause types</u>
Clause and sentence complexity increases over the three texts. Text 1 is almost exclusively composed of main clauses co-ordinated by *and*. Clause connectives are limited, with only one use of *then*. There is a single subordinate clause: *when we got there*.

Connectives

By contrast, the writer of Text 2 uses a variety of conjunctions, both co-ordinating (*and, so, but*) and subordinating (*because*). This allows the writer to indicate cause and effect and reason in the relationships between clauses. There is therefore a greater percentage of complex as opposed to compound sentences, although the writer of Text 1 does not use punctuation, so sentence units are not identified and cannot readily be compared. Text 3 uses the subordinating conjunctions *when* and *as*, and uses not only two-clause sentences but multiple-clause sentences with relative clauses embedded. (*I twisted the rusty key in the lock and it snapped against my skin as I placed the rubber band which it was attached to over my wrist.*) This writer also uses indirect reported speech within an embedded clause: *they had*

Subordination

agreed that they would meet me in the pool. The majority of the sentence types in Text 3 are complex sentences, although the writer also uses simple one-clause sentences for immediate effect: *This was going to be fun.*

Connectives also increase, from just *then* in Text 1, to *instead* and *suddenly* in Text 2, to *Moments before* and the use of *with a single shudder* in Text 3.

> Pupils can be encouraged to address issues such as increasing the use of connectives to make meaning more explicit while editing and re-drafting their writing.

Feedback

Complexity of phrase development

The complexity of noun phrases deserves some further comment. In the feedback to Task C5 we noted that noun phrases can contain single words or long strings of words. In advertising text, noun phrases can be very long indeed because of the heavy embedded post-modification of the head noun. For example, in the noun phrase:

an attractive vehicle with inbuilt stereo CD with all around sound

the head noun, *vehicle*, is qualified by the prepositional phrase *with inbuilt stereo*, which is itself qualified by another prepositional phrase. Expanding the noun phrase in this way, or by extending the pre-modification of the noun with adverbs and adjectives, as in:

an extremely sleek, sporty and amazingly attractive vehicle

is one way of expanding sentences. A simple two-word noun phrase, such as *a vehicle*, can be expanded by pre- and post-modifying the noun:

NOUN PHRASE STRUCTURE		
PRE-MODIFICATION	HEAD NOUN	POST-MODIFICATION
an extremely sleek, sporty and amazingly attractive	*vehicle*	*with inbuilt stereo CD with all around sound*

Post-modification of nouns in noun phrases can be in the form of prepositional phrases (as above) and defining relative clauses (as below). This causes some difficulty in our description of syntax having a hierarchy of units, since we said that clause is at a higher level than phrase. The post-modification of nouns in noun phrases is an exception. Defining relative clauses are used to qualify nouns in the same way as the prepositional phrases seen in the example above. In the examples below, the noun is qualified by a defining relative clause:

> Non-defining relative clauses are true clauses, though. The difference is explained below in the feedback to Task C8 – Grammar and punctuation.

NOUN PHRASE STRUCTURE		
PRE-MODIFICATION	HEAD NOUN	POST-MODIFICATION
an extremely sleek, sporty and amazingly attractive	*vehicle*	*which outruns the opposition*
the	*clanking*	*that came from below me* (Text 3)

Variety of clause types

Teaching and assessing pupils will involve you in planning for and assessing their development as writers. They should be able to write narrative and non-narrative text that uses complex sentences and a range of connectives to convey with precision complex semantic

Post-modification (margin)

Pre-modification (margin)

Complex semantic relationships (margin)

relationships such as cause and effect, reason, sequence, purpose and condition. A range is represented in the writing of Texts 2 and 3:

Reason

condition   cause
[*Mark was really excited*]   [***because** they were going on a plane.*]

Sequence

first   second
[***When** I got out of the lift,*]   [*I made my way towards the reception desk.*]

Purpose

problem   solution
[*I was totally fed up,*]   ***so***   [*I decided it was time to take advantage of the hotel swimming pool.*]

Concession

condition   concession
[*Mark was a pretty normal boy*]   ***but***   [*he was never really happy.*]

Implicit and explicit semantic relationships

The writer of Text 1, however, fails to make explicit the relationships between clauses, although implicit relationships of sequence can be inferred by the organization of the text. In addition, reason is implied in:

> *we went to the hide-out and we saw the birds and it was good*

If we rearrange the sentence and insert an appropriate conjunction, this makes explicit the implied reason:

condition   reason
[*It was good*]   [***because** we went to the hide-out and saw the birds.*]

> Writers can be encouraged to make explicit the implicit semantic relationships between clauses during writing, editing and redrafting of texts.

Use of a wide range of subordinating and co-ordinating conjunctions and connectives (such as *initially*, *consequently*) or nouns (such as *reason, effect, purpose*) will increase the variety and complexity of clause types and functions. Pupils can also be encouraged to expand sentences by inserting relative and non-finite clauses and by combining simple sentences to make compound and complex sentences, where appropriate.

Action

Marking guides for Key Stage 2 and 3 end-of-key-stage tests give examples of the kind of sentence types and structures one expects at each National Curriculum level in relation to sample texts. Examine previous tests in detail after making yourself familiar with the terminology for description. QCA (Qualifications and Curriculum Authority) and SEAC (Schools Examination and Assessment Council) publish books covering National Curriculum issues. For example:

> SEAC (1992) *Pupils' Work Assessed – Key Stage 3: English*. SEAC.

Task C7 – Standard and non-standard grammar

Answers

Grammatical errors

In the answers below, the correction is highlighted in bold.
(a) The **children's** party will take place in the Dining Hall today between 2.00 and 3.30 p.m.
(b) The incidences of speeding recorded over the past year on this stretch of road **have** increased, if we compare the statistics with the previous 12 months.

> (b) Verbal agreement with a plural noun.

(c)   'You should **have** seen him run the 200 metres,' said Mary to her friend Ann at the school's Sports Day.

(d)   The pupils were in the classroom at lunch time, when they know **they're** not allowed to be in the form rooms.

(e)   However, things did not go as **easily** as expected.

(f)   Team membership allows pupils to develop confidence and show a sense of pride in the community in which they have become a part ~~of~~.

(g)   I bought a Jaguar. It was the best car I had ever **driven**.

(h)   The test was ~~more~~ easier than I expected.

(i)   I had hoped for **fewer** interruptions.

(j)   Throughout history schools, and the way they teach pupils, **have** changed.

(k)   There **are** three stages of school: infant, junior and secondary.

(l)   On the other hand there **were** many positive aspects to my education.

(m)   Their basic skills of writing **need** to be worked on.

(n)   The songs which we listened to on the radio **were** relaxing.

(o)   I saw him quite **clearly** through my binoculars.

(p)   The girls did very **well** in the netball tournament.

(q)   He drives **dangerously** on the motorway.

(c) Misapplication of auxiliary verb with preposition *of*.

(d) Homophone error – see feedback to Task C8.

(f) Unnecessary second preposition.

(g) Past participle, not simple past tense.

(h) Two comparatives.

(i) Singular noun uses *less*; plural uses *fewer*.

When non-standard speech features are transferred to writing they become errors in standard written English.

As a teacher of English, one part of your job will be to make children aware of language variation. Another part will be to be aware yourself, and to help pupils to be aware, of how to write clearly and accurately in standard English and be able to identify common errors.

Differences between speech and writing are another issue. See feedback to Task E1.

Non-standard grammar and vocabulary

(r)   <u>Non-standard grammar and vocabulary</u>

1.   Use of present instead of past tense – *says* for *said* (line 1); *come* for *came* (lines 6 and 10).

2.   Pronoun usage – use of object pronoun *her* in subject position rather than *she* (line 1); use of interrogative pronoun *what* instead of relative pronoun *that* or *which* (line 10).

3.   *the finish* used rather than *the end* (line 2).

4.   Number agreement – *they was* rather than *they were* – third person singular rather than third person plural (lines 4 and 7).

5.   Double negative – *you did**n't** get **nothing** out of it* (line 5); ***never** spent **no** money* (line 9).

6.   Use of *wireless* indicates speaker is of a certain age (line 6).

6.   Double object – *he couldn't understand **it why they couldn't** **score at home*** (lines 7–8).

7.   Reduced verb phrase – *they **got** a lot of local talent* (lines 9 and 10) – auxiliary *have* omitted.

Feedback

In (r) you may have commented on other features that are spontaneous features of speech or colloquialisms rather than non-standard grammar. It is important to recognize the difference between informal speech features and non-standard grammar. Items like *er, you know, I mean, like* are determined by the informality of the register. Similarly, repetitions and non-sequiturs are common features of speech. If you transcribe any piece of speech from a tape recording, you will find these present in even the most well-planned speeches.

Differences between speech and writing

Writers such as Hardy, Fowles and Salinger use non-standard speech in their narratives, and more recently the novel and popular film *Trainspotting* has used non-standard dialect. In the following extract from Fowles's *The French Lieutenant's Woman*, non-standard Cockney dialect is written for Charles's manservant, Sam.

Non-standard speech in narrative

> 'If you goes on a-standin' in the hair, sir, you won't, neither.'
> His master gave him a dry look. He and Sam had been together for

four years and knew each other rather better than the partners in many
a supposedly more intimate menage.

5   'Sam, you've been drinking again.'
    'No, sir.'
    'The new room is better?'
    'Yes, sir.'
    'And the commons?'
10   'Very hacceptable, sir.'
    'Quod est demonstrandum. *You have the hump of a morning*
that would make a miser sing. Ergo, *you have been drinking.'*
    ...
    'It's that there kitchen-girl's at Mrs Tranter's, sir. I ain't 'alf going
to ...'
    'Kindly put that instrument down. And explain yourself.'
15   'I sees her. Dahn out there.' He jerked his thumb at the window.
'Right across the street she calls.'
    'And what did she call, pray?'

(CHAPTER 7)

Fowles's narrator labels Sam as a 'snob' – one of the class of 'new young prosperous artisans and would-be superior domestics' whose 'struggle with the aspirate' was 'more frequently lost than won' – and then comments:

But his wrong a's and h's were not really comic; they were signs of a social revolution, and this was something Charles failed to recognize.

The struggle with the aspirate is only one of the features of the Cockney dialect used here and relates to phonology rather than grammar. You should, though, be able to identify number disagreement (line 1), the present for past tense (lines 15 and 16) and use of double negative (line 1) common to the extract used in the task.

Action
Drawing pupils' attention to their own non-standard usage needs to be done sensitively. A way of doing this, whilst also developing your own understanding and recognition of its features, is to examine the speech of characters in soap operas. Since different dialects have different grammatical and lexical features, you can also examine the combination of grammatical features that characterize a particular dialect.

'Coronation Street', 'Brookside', 'Eastenders' and other television programmes, such as 'Rab C. Nesbit', have some characters who use non-standard dialects.

You can also examine the use of dialect in literature, as suggested above. Pupils may then be ready to examine features of their own dialect, so that a study of the grammatical features of dialect is analytical rather than critical. You can then move on to the question of eradicating dialect features from standard written English and the consideration of when non-standard forms are appropriate in writing.

Task C8 – Grammar and punctuation

Answers

Comma usage is coded using superscript numbers:
[1] comma used for clause boundary in complex sentence
[2] commas used for list of nouns (or adjectives)
[3] commas used for appositional noun phrase

4 commas around non-defining relative clause which interrupts main clause

5 commas not used around the relative clause in this sentence, indicating that this is a defining relative clause and that only the 'desserts that have a higher sugar content' are being referred to

(a) My diet excludes butter,[2] chips,[2] ice cream and chocolate.

(b) Fat,[3] especially saturated fat,[3] should be carefully controlled.

(c) When low fat margarine is used,[1] it should be sparingly applied.

(d) Vegetables,[4] which can be eaten freely,[4] contain many essential vitamins.

(e) Desserts [5] that have a higher sugar content [5] should be avoided.

> Commas are often misused in pupils' writing.

Colon and semi-colon

In the following sentences the appropriate mark – colon or semi-colon – has been inserted with the underscore.

(f) *Debbie dropped her bag and out spilled the contents:_a large bunch of keys;_her husband's wallet that he had asked her to keep;_a calculator for the shopping and a rather crumpled handkerchief.*

(g) *They talked all day without mentioning the one topic on their minds:_the robbery.*

(h) *I once had a Jaguar car;_it was the best I had ever driven.*

(i) *The sun shone;_the birds sang;_I was happy.*

Apostrophe

Apostrophes have been inserted in the following sentences:

Possession apostrophe

(j) *The **children's** teacher arrived in the classroom to begin the day.*
The possession apostrophe is inserted before the *s*, because *children* is an irregular plural. Possessive plurals usually involve the addition of an *s* (*dog, dogs*), but there are some exceptions (*child, child**ren**; woman, wo**men***). The misconception arises here because a plural is recognized and the usual rule is to insert the apostrophe after the *s*.

(k) ***Women's** fiction is a popular area of study on degree courses.*
The explanation for the insertion of the apostrophe is the same as for *children*. *Women* is an irregular plural.

Omission apostrophe

(l) ***I'll** be coming home at 4.30 today.*
Omission apostrophes are more rarely missed. *I'll* is the contracted form of *I will* with the apostrophe denoting the missing letters. The commonest mistake of this kind is with *they're* being written as *there*. In this case pupils are failing to recognize that a contraction is being used and mistaking the word *there* for the contracted *they are*, the two being homophones in some speech.

Homophone

(m) *The **dog's** dinner looked very unappetizing to me.*

(n) *We were completely exhausted at the end of our **day's** exploration.*
As with (m), ***days'*** would be acceptable. It depends whether a singular or plural day is intended.

> It is unlikely that two dogs would be sharing one dinner, but, if so, *dogs'* would be acceptable.

(o) Correct sentences are:

***Bill's** Mum gave me a lift to school.*   ***It's** a nice day.*
*The **train's** brakes failed.*   *The dog ate **its** dinner.*
*The **windows** are looking dirty.*

The problems with the incorrect sentences are as follows:

1. The possession apostrophe is missing:
   ***Bills** Mum gave me a lift to school.*
   *The **trains** brakes failed.*

2. The omission apostrophe is missing:
   ***Its** a nice day today*

Omission apostrophes are not so frequently missed as possession apostrophes but are missed with *It's*, because this can also be a word: *its*. Knowledge of word class helps here. *It + is* (*It's*) comprises a pronoun and verb, whereas *its* is a possessive adjective or determiner.

> It is common for writers to miss out the apostrophe of possession completely. One could almost say that it is so common that the possession apostrophe is dying out in English usage.

3. Insertion of a possession apostrophe where none is needed:
   *The dog ate **it's** dinner.*
   *The **window's** are looking dirty.*

No apostrophe is needed in either example. *Its* is already possessive, being a possessive adjective like *his, her, their*. It needs no apostrophe to signal it, although you will come across incorrect usage such as *it's* or *its'*. *Windows* is a plural noun; there is no possession here. Some pupils insert apostrophes before or after the plural morpheme -*s*.

> It will be useful to these pupils to point out the difference between the plural morpheme -*s* and the possessive morpheme '*s*. There are two different meanings here, one of number and one of belonging.

Feedback

Comma

From the examples we can see that commas are used for a number of purposes:
- for lists of nouns and adjectives
- to mark appositional noun phrases
- around non-defining relative clauses
- to mark clause boundaries within complex sentences

In addition, they are used:
- to mark the clause boundary in written speech, to separate the speech from the reporting clause:
  She said, 'Stop!'. 'I can't,' said Sue.
- after sentence adverbs:
  ***Accordingly,** when she retired at night, she asked the chambermaid ...*
- in the writing of tag questions:
  That's the last one, isn't it?
- for interruptions by another clause or phrase:
  This, then, is the answer.
  This, she interrupted, is the answer.
  The answer is not, by any stretch of the imagination, easy.

> Commas are not usually used for clause boundaries in sentences where main clauses are linked; a semi-colon is used here. See page 66.

They are not used:
- around defining relative clauses
- before *and*, although there are instances when this convention will not be applied, for instance, when you want that part of the sentence to be separate

The use of commas to mark grammatical boundaries in sentences is governed by syntax, so knowledge of grammar is important if commas are going to be used correctly. They are commonly misused where full stops or at least a semi-colon is necessary.

Possessive adjective

Plural noun

Comma

Full stop

Full stop

Full stops are used for:
- abbreviations (*Mr., G.C.S.E., N.B.*)
- the end of sentences

One of the problems experienced by pupils is deciding what is and what is not a sentence. We have already noted that speech uses truncated sentences; some written genres, notably advertising and poetry, also use stylistic sentences that are not grammatically complete. These are exceptions to the rule.

- generally, fully grammatical sentences must contain a finite verb in a main clause

The following cannot be sentences in standard written English:
- non-finite clauses: *Exhausted by the climb, ...*
- finite subordinate clauses: *When we had eaten dinner, ...*

However, exceptions are made:
- in the representation of written speech
- where there is ellipsis:
    'Are you coming for dinner on Sunday?'
    'No, I'm not.' (ellipsis of verb)

> Pupils often use commas where full stops or semi-colons are needed.

Semi-colon

Semi-colon

Semi-colons are often misused. They are sometimes similar to commas and sometimes like full stops.

They are used like a comma:
- in lists where the items are phrases, rather than single words

They are used like a full stop:
- to separate linked main clauses to indicate a relationship between them where a full stop would otherwise be used:
    The business of life was to get her daughters married; its solace was visiting and news. (MRS BENNET, IN *PRIDE AND PREJUDICE*)

Semi-colons are not usually used to separate subordinate and main clauses in a sentence, a comma being more appropriate here.

Colon

Colon

Colons are used:
- to indicate a list of following items or where a simple item follows
- before a quotation or speech in a play script

Apostrophe

Apostrophe

There are two kinds of apostrophe: apostrophes of possession and of omission.

Possession apostrophe

Possession apostrophes indicate the possessive case.
e.g.
1. *He forgot about the dog's dinner* (singular possessive – the dinner belongs to one dog).
2. *The soldiers' letters were sent home from the war* (plural possessive – the letters belong to the soldiers).
3. *They heard their children's screams as they disappeared into the Ghost Train at the fair* (plural possessive – the screams belong to a group of children. *Children* is an irregular plural noun – it is not formed using the plural morpheme -*s*).

> Apostrophes of possession and omission are often misused in pupils' writing. Although pupils begin to use apostrophes in Key Stage 1 or 2, misconceptions and misuses are common, even into adulthood. It will be necessary to reinforce knowledge and teach some pupils that apostrophes come in two kinds and are used for different purposes.

Possession apostrophes are used with nouns.

Omission apostrophe

Omission apostrophes indicate where a letter or letters are omitted, as in *isn't*, *I'll*, *o'clock*. They involve the joining of at least two words from a variety of word classes – *o'clock* is a contraction of *on the clock*.

Dashes and brackets

Dashes and brackets

Pairs of dashes and brackets are used for additional, often illustrative, information or asides.

Single dashes are used very much like colons:

> *There are two types of apostrophe – possession and omission.*

In this case, the colon and dash might also be used.

> *There are two types of apostrophe:– possession and omission.*

Action

The ITTNC states: 'Trainees must be taught how to teach punctuation, including how to: a. use well-written texts to demonstrate the function of different punctuation marks and how they should be used, *e.g. looking at the use of the semi-colon and the colon.*' In order to improve your subject knowledge in this area, examine well-written academic and pupil text books and non-fiction. You can also examine literature, but you need to be aware when using literature and some non-fiction with pupils that poets, novelists and advertising copywriters abandon or play with standard punctuation for stylistic and communicative effect. However, this in itself is an interesting and fruitful area of analysis.

Punctuation and style

Section D:

The textual system of written language

Task D1 – Textual cohesion

Answers

(a) Reference – 1, 3, 4, 5, 6, 12, 19, 26
(b) Substitution – 18
(c) Ellipsis – 14, 17, 22
(d) Conjunction – 7, 20, 25
(e) Lexical cohesion – 2, 6, 8, 9, 10, 11, 13, 15, 23, 24, 27, 28, 29

Some of the cohesive ties are of two kinds. For example, number six, *their route*, refers back to *their direct road*, with *route* and *road* being lexical reiteration through the use of a synonym. In addition, the possessive *their* refers back to the three members of the party. There will be more examples of dual cohesion than are indicated in the answers. In some cases one selection has been made.

(f) The cohesive tie over the largest stretch of text in the extract is with 23: *she was again applied to* is referring back, through lexical repetition and pronominal reference, to *Elizabeth was applied to for her approbation*, at the end of the first paragraph. However, the mention of *Pemberley*, in the first paragraph of this extract from the end of chapter 42, has links that span enormous stretches of previous text. Just looking part of the way back through the text, the following links are found:

> previous lexical link: three paragraphs earlier in chapter 42
> previous lexical link: 35 pages earlier in chapter 35
> previous lexical link: 40 pages earlier in chapter 25

The Jane Austen website allows you to search keywords in e-texts of her novels.

Feedback
Halliday and Hasan's (1976) description of cohesion was briefly explained with reference to each of their categories in the feedback to Task C4 on intra-sentential cohesion. The same resources are used to create textual cohesion, although these items will be referring across larger stretches of text. Anaphoric reference and lexical cohesion are clearly the predominant kinds of cohesion in this extract.

Intra-sentential cohesion

Lexical cohesion

Reference

Example 1 uses the personal pronoun *they* and the possessive determiner *their* to refer anaphorically to the three members of the party, who have been introduced prior to this extract. Example 3, *her aunt* refers back to *Mrs Gardiner* in the first line and to *Elizabeth* (in the same sentence). The reader already knows, from preceding text, that Mrs Gardiner is Elizabeth's aunt. Examples 4 and 5 refer back to *Pemberley*.

Refer back to the text on pages 19 and 20.

Examples 12 and 19 exhibit demonstrative reference. *There* refers to Pemberley, which is not in their immediate proximity, and *this* refers to the idea of Elizabeth speaking to her aunt, which she has just thought of. Here the proximity is not of an object to a person, as in 12, but in the proximity of a phrase to the demonstrative item.

Substitution

Example 18, *such a risk*, is clearly substitution of the clause *of meeting Mr Darcy, while viewing the place* by the word *such*, although Halliday and Hasan list substitution through the use of *so, do, not, the same*.

Ellipsis

In example 14 we see ellipsis of the words *great houses*, used earlier in the sentence, to avoid repetition. Example 17, *the very idea*, uses lexical cohesion to link the word *idea* with *possibility*, two lines before, but ellipses the clause *of meeting Mr Darcy, while viewing the place*. Example 22 is skilfully elliptical on the part of Jane Austen; *the subject*, although recoverable from the text as being the proposed visit to Pemberley, is also for the reader the subject with which Elizabeth is preoccupied: the possibility of meeting Mr Darcy again. Mrs Gardiner, unlike the reader, is unaware of this particular subject. We can see here how cohesive properties help create intrigue for the reader in terms of the cohesive semantics within the text and in the process of reading and the relationship between reader, narrator and text.

Conjunction

There are clearly many more conjunctive ties than have been labelled for this task. The three that have been selected contribute to the temporal sequence and flow of the text. *Accordingly,* for example is a temporal adverb in that it relies on the decision Elizabeth has already made, in the previous paragraph. It also establishes a causal

Conjunction

Temporal
Causal

relationship between the things that Elizabeth was worrying about and the subsequent action of discussing the issues with the chambermaid.

Additive and adversative

There are many additive and adversative conjunctions in the extract, in the use of *and, nor,* and *but.*

Lexical cohesion

Lexical Cohesion

There are many lexical links in this extract through the vocabulary used. Halliday and Hasan describe lexical cohesion as the processes of reiteration and collocation of vocabulary. Reiteration involves direct repetition of vocabulary and the use of semantic relationships of synonymy and antonymy (and hyponymy) between lexical items. Semantic relations of synonymy and antonymy are not always created through the use of direct items; the relationships are established through contrast, opposition and similarity of words and phrases.

> This involves knowledge of the semantic relations discussed in the feedback to Task B2.

Reiteration

Collocation

Collocation involves the co-occurrence of words, so that the words *grounds, carpets* and *curtains* are predictable collocates of *house.*

The table below classifies the cohesion by reiteration among the selected examples.

LEXICAL COHESION BY REITERATION		
REPETITION	**SYNONYMY**	**ANTONYMY**
• 2: *Lambton* – lines 4 and 1. • 11: *the place* – lines 9, 7. • 15: *fine* – paragraphs 4 and 3. (It is also synonymous with *great* in para. 3.) • 23: *applied to* – paragraphs 6 and 1. • 27: *Pemberley Woods* – chapters 43 and 42.	• 6: *route* – *steps* (line 3) *road* (line 5) *route* (line 6). • 8 and 11: *the place* – *Pemberley* (line 4) *the place* (lines 7 and 9 and thereafter through repetition of *Pemberley* and use of *house, place* and *it*). • 9 and 10: *willingness, inclination* and *approbation* are used synonymously. • 13: *disinclination* is used synonymously with *no pleasure* and *distressed*, through the use of negation.	• 13: *disinclination* is an antonym of *inclination* and *willingness*. • 24: *not really any dislike to the scheme* is contrasted with *obliged to show a disinclination for seeing it.* • 28: *perturbation* is contrasted with *indifference* (but is also synonymous with *spirits in a high flutter*).

Example 21, *the last question*, does not appear to fall neatly into any of Halliday and Hasan's categories. *Last* would fit into the category of temporal conjunction, but the phrase refers anaphorically, through the use of the definite article and the discourse label, *question*, to the last part of the preceding item of indirect speech.

Sophisticated reading strategies are needed here in order to understand the significance of this semantic link. Within the previous sentence there are three items of indirect reported speech in the form of indirect questions. It is to the last, and most disturbing question for Elizabeth, that Jane Austen is referring: *whether the family were down for the summer.* Francis (1994) has looked at the phenomenon of nouns, such as *question*, which 'retrospectively label' earlier words and phrases. The term

Anaphoric noun

'anaphoric noun' or 'retrospective label' serves this example well, describing the reference through the use of a noun rather than a pronoun. *The last question* is not self-sufficient in terms of meaning; its meaning can only be understood with reference to the preceding text.

Cohesion in non-fiction

Action

This task focuses on cohesion in fiction. To increase your knowledge of how cohesion works across sentences and paragraphs in non-fiction, look at a range of non-fiction texts, such as:

- an advertisement in a magazine
- a page from an encyclopaedia in a book and on CD-ROM
- a page on an Internet web site
- a recipe or the rules for a board game

For each text, carry out a cohesive analysis similar to the one done in this task, locating examples of each of the five types of cohesion.

The texts below contain a comprehensive coverage of aspects of cohesion.

The key text in the study of cohesion is:

> Halliday, M. A. K. and Hasan, R. (1976) *Cohesion in English.* Longman.

The following text is a useful study on the nature of reading development and understanding of the cohesive properties of text:

> Chapman, J. (1983) *Reading Development and Cohesion.* Heinemann Educational.

Francis's description of labelling can be found in:

> Coulthard, M. (ed.) (1994) *Advances in Written Text Analysis.* Routledge.

An interesting study on lexical chains in text is:

> Hoey, M. P. (1991) *Patterns of Lexis in Text.* Oxford University Press.

This book develops Halliday and Hasan's ideas of lexical cohesion through collocation and reiteration. Particularly useful is the idea of lexical chains that run through a text contributing to comprehension and the building of themes and central ideas in fiction and non-fiction. The reiteration of *Pemberley* throughout *Pride and Prejudice* is an example of this. Chapman (1983) also discusses lexical reiteration.

Task D2 – Text structure, form and genre

Answers

Form

(a) sonnet
(b) ballad
(c) nursery rhyme, limerick or song
(d) jingle or octet
(e) heroic couplets or rhyming couplets
(f) *haiku*
(g) see the feedback below

Feedback

Sonnet

(a) Although consisting of the characteristic 14 lines of iambic pentameter, in this sonnet Keats experiments with the rhyme scheme. The 'abab cdcd bc efef' arrangement, the punctuation at the end of the eighth line and the corresponding separation of content into the two sections, make this most like the Petrarchan sonnet with its octet and sestet.

Ballad

(b) This extract consisting of the first four stanzas of Keats's well-known ballad has many of the features one would expect: four-line stanzas; an uncomplicated rhyme scheme with two of the four lines rhyming; simple language; a story with a tragic theme; repetition and meter which makes it song-like.

Nursery rhyme

(c) This has a rhyme scheme and rhythm akin to a limerick or nursery rhyme, reminiscent of 'Little Jack Horner' or 'Little Miss Muffet', with the feminine rhyme and 'aabccb' pattern.

Jingle

(d) This has many of the hallmarks of a jingle: a catchy rhythm and strong feminine rhyme on which one focuses rather than on meaning.

Heroic couplet

(e) The heroic couplet is made up of rhyming pairs of lines with iambic pentameter, as in this extract.

Haiku

(f) The *haiku*, originating from Japan, consists of three lines of five, seven and five syllables respectively. It expresses a single idea.

Genre

(g) The two genres are described below and on the following page. Each description contains a bulleted list of typically ordered features of the genre and its key linguistic or presentational components.

'Junk' mail letter

<u>The 'junk' mail or persuasive letter</u>
Refer back to the letter on page 22 to locate the following:
- conventional opening, with *dear* plus the name, rather than *madam*, to make a personal appeal; positive and complimentary tone

Persuasion

- 'buttering up' section, accentuating the potential client's importance and fortunate position, using phrases such as *valued guest, delighted to offer you, opportunity, being offered*
- points out choice, amenities and outstanding features, using long noun phrases so distinctive of advertising and brochures: *a four star Georgian hotel set in 262 acres with its own 18 hole golf course*
- conditional clause(s) plus consequence: *if* + action = beneficial effect
- imperative clause(s) telling the reader what to do to take advantage of this wonderful opportunity
- free gift
- solutions to any problems: *it's simple to book*
- optimistic closing, supposing that you are now sold on the idea
- high profile imperative, reiterating what to do to take advantage of the opportunity, in large bold letters

Linguistic and presentational features:
- use of bold font and capitals to highlight key phrases and sentences
- use of modal verbs (*will*)
- use of imperative and conditional clauses to persuade
- short paragraphs to accentuate points
- listing of benefits, using complex noun phrases and positive adjectives (*valued, splendid, fabulous, superb, plenty, magnificent, great, free, simple, happy*), many of which are synonyms of each other
- a problem-solving approach

Novel 'blurb'

<u>The blurb on the back of a novel</u>
There will usually be a house style for the blurb on the back of a novel, but some of the following features are expected:
- a one-sentence summary of the story in bold above the précis, to help a potential reader in the selection process; these statements can be quickly scanned by readers in shops

- a précis of the plot in a single paragraph, giving the reader a preview
- a critical summary of what the author is attempting in the novel, giving the reader an indication of the message and viewpoints
- sound bites from reviews by major critics or leading newspapers, in praise of the author, style or novel, which give credibility
- photograph of the author, which helps the reader identify with the writer
- price and bar code, for the retailer
- ISBN for recording and ordering purposes
- publisher's name
- the genre of the book, to help the reader choose and the retailer categorize
- *'cover illustration by ...'*

Linguistic and presentational features:
- a variety of fonts, colours and layout
- high degree of nominal and adjectival descriptive, evaluative terms

You may not find these features in exactly the same order in all texts of these types, but these typical generic features could be used as a template for other texts.

Writing frames

The study of genre can help in the production of frames and structures for use in the writing or comprehension of texts. Writing frames and generic formulae have been developed by Australian applied linguists to support pupils' writing. The ITTNC states that we should provide the opportunity for 'pupils to write in different forms ... through providing examples and teaching pupils how to analyse them for their linguistic and other conventions' and 'using structured approaches to support pupils' first attempts, e.g. writing frames'.

Some useful texts that explain and develop the notion of genre and writing frames, particularly for non-fiction, are listed in the **Action** on pages 73 and 74.

Narrative structures

Labov (1972), Longacre (1983) and Propp (1958) have also contributed to genre theory in their structural descriptions of narrative. The tables below and on page 73 show Labov's (1972) and Longacre's (1983) descriptions of narrative structure. It is important to note that all the structural components will not necessarily be found in a single narrative. Both are attempts to describe the typical elements of narrative.

Labov developed his description in relation to spoken narrative, but it can be used for written narratives too.

> Martin (1989) describes genres through formulae. The essay is reduced to:
>
> *thesis$\wedge$argument$^n\wedge$ restatement of thesis*
>
> where $\wedge$ indicates movement to another stage and ^{n} denotes the possibility of a number of these elements.

LABOV'S NARRATIVE STRUCTURE		
STRUCTURAL PARTS	**PARTS AS ANSWERS TO QUESTIONS**	**SUMMARY OF CONTENTS**
ABSTRACT	What is the narrative is about?	A summary of the whole story; sometimes an evaluation of it.
ORIENTATION	Who, when, what, where?	Time, place, people, their activity or situation. The orientation may all be at the beginning of the narrative, or at strategic points later on.

LABOV'S NARRATIVE STRUCTURE (CONTINUED)		
STRUCTURAL PARTS	PARTS AS ANSWERS TO QUESTIONS	SUMMARY OF CONTENTS
COMPLICATING ACTION	Then what happened?	An event, or series of events, temporally ordered. (An essential element.)
EVALUATION	So what?	Used by the narrator to indicate the point of the narrative. (Can be found throughout.)
RESULT or RESOLUTION	What finally happened?	The termination of the series of events.
CODA		Indication of end; general observations; bridging the gap between narrative and reality.

Episodic structure

Longacre's description identifies a more complex episodic structure that includes:

- surface structure and features (i.e. what can be observed on the page)
- notional structure or plot and its function in the narrative

LONGACRE'S NARRATIVE STRUCTURE			
SURFACE STRUCTURE	SURFACE FEATURES	NOTIONAL STRUCTURE: PLOT	FUNCTION
TITLE		[Surface features only]	
APERTURE	Opening; formulaic phrase	[Surface features only]	
STAGE	Expository paragraph/ chapter(s)	1. Exposition	'Lay it out'
EPISODES (Pre-Peak)	Paragraphs or chapters containing sequential episodes	2. Inciting moment 3. Developing conflict	'Get something going' 'Keep the heat on'
PEAK	Peak episode, emphasized by: • concentration of participants • heightened vividness • change of pace • change of vantage point or orientation	4. Climax 5. Dénouement	'Knot it all up properly' 'Loosen it'
EPISODES (Post-Peak)	Further episodes	(5. Dénouement) 6. Final suspense	('Loosen it') 'Keep untangling'
CLOSURE	Variety of features, but may include a moral	7. Conclusion	'Wrap it up'
FINIS	Closure; formulaic phrase	[Surface features only]	

Action

Develop your ability to analyse genre by examining further texts in the way demonstrated here, and be prepared to model the writing of different genres. Ask a friend to tell you a story about something that happened to them and try to analyse the story's structure using Labov's description. Examine a short narrative, such as a children's traditional tale, and analyse its structure according to Longacre's more complex structure or after looking at Propp (below).

Some useful writers on the subject are:

> Cope, B. and Kalantzis, M. (eds.) (1993) *The Powers of Literacy: A Genre Approach to Teaching Writing*. Falmer Press.
> Lewis, M. and Wray, D. (1996) *Developing Children's Non-Fiction Writing*. Scholastic.
> Lewis, M. and Wray, D. (1997) *Extending Literacy: Children Reading and Writing Non-Fiction*. Routledge.
> Martin, J. (1989) *Factual Writing: Exploring and Challenging Social Reality*. Oxford University Press.
> Propp, V. (1958) *Morphology of the Folktale*. University of Texas Press.

> Lewis and Wray write for the primary school, but much of their work is also appropriate for Key Stage 3.

Section E:

Language as a social, cultural and historical phenomenon

Written and spoken English

Task E1 – Written versus spoken English

Answers

Answers are given in the table below.

SPEECH	WRITING
uses tag questions uses truncated sentences uses hesitation markers uses core vocabulary, rather than a broad range sentences are mainly compound and simple	uses a range of sentence and clause types uses long complex noun phrases uses cohesion to avoid repetition has a range of subordinating conjunctions uses few signals of interaction

Feedback

A number of the key features of speech and writing are focused on in the task. A fuller list of features is shown in the table below, which is arranged in pairs with the left-and right-hand statements being complementary.

Features of speech and writing

SPOKEN LANGUAGE	WRITTEN LANGUAGE
has inexplicit words or sentences carries audible marks of boundaries use of language is sensitive to audience uses interaction markers and checks uses slang and colloquialisms has more than one participant uses gesture and non-verbal signals revises and corrects in mid-sentence co-ordinates clauses mainly with *and* and *but* is spontaneous and composed quickly sentences mainly compound and simple often concerned with social relations uses few complex sentences or subordinate clauses	words are carefully contextualized has no audible marks for boundaries few allowances are made for audience uses few signals of interaction uses technical and semi-technical terms carried out individually narrates body language and thought errors can be eliminated later has a range of subordinating conjunctions takes time to compose uses more complex sentences often transmits information uses a range of sentence and clause types

> You may be able to think of other features of speech and writing not included here.

Spoken language *(continued)*	Written language *(continued)*
uses repetition	uses cohesion to avoid repetition
few uses of passives	uses greater number of passives
ephemeral	permanent
uses core vocabulary items	uses a broad range of vocabulary
feedback is given immediately	feedback takes time or is not given
uses hesitation markers	the time taken in writing avoids hesitation
uses truncated sentences	uses complete grammatical sentences
uses simple noun phrases	uses long, complex noun phrases
uses tag questions	tags are redundant, but may be stylistic
unless recorded cannot be recalled sufficiently for detailed analysis	can be analysed in detail

Generalizing

Differentiation between speech and writing

You may not completely agree with the way that the features have been divided between written and spoken language, but if we are to isolate features we need to be able to generalize. For instance, simple noun phrases or tag questions are found in writing but are most characteristic of speech. Additionally, pupils whose writing has not moved far from speech towards a differentiated written form will use many of the spoken features in their writing: simple noun phrases, slang and colloquialisms, few complex sentences and subordinate clauses and core vocabulary items.

Audience

You may also want to argue with some of the distinctions. For example, to say that speakers are sensitive to audience and writers are not is far too simplistic. We will all have come across speakers who are unable to accommodate a particular audience's needs in terms of its age or the degree of formality required. Equally, writers often make careful considerations of the needs of the audience, and as teachers we encourage pupils to do this. The audience is not as immediate, however, with writing, and when we write we do not receive instant feedback in the way we do as speakers.

Speech in the novel

There are additional features to the ones indicated here. For example, novelists who write dialogue for their characters omit many of the features of real speech: overlaps, hesitation markers, revisions and truncated sentences. Jane Austen's characters are inordinately articulate, even bearing in mind their social status and education!

Nominalization

One of the features that distinguishes academic technical writing is the nominalization of verbs. For example, if we locate the verbs in the following sentence, we can then nominalize them to produce a more complex sentence:

> Novelists who **write** dialogue for their characters **omit** many of the features of real speech: overlaps, hesitation markers, revisions and truncated sentences. This is a widespread phenomenon.

Becomes:

> **The omission** of many of the features of real speech – overlaps, hesitation markers, revisions and truncated sentences – is a widespread phenomenon among novelists who write dialogue for their characters.

or:

> **In the writing** of dialogues for their characters, novelists' **omission** of the features of real speech – overlaps, hesitation markers, revisions and truncated sentences – is a widespread phenomenon.

In the transformed examples, one sentence carries the meaning of the original two.

Condensation

When this is done, communication of the processes, which is usually done through the verbs, is done by the nominal groups and the verb becomes the verb 'to be' (*is* and *are*, in the two examples above), which carries little meaning. The process of nominalization also allows sentences to be condensed.

Some style guides encourage writers to avoid nominalization, because it obfuscates.

Action
Look at pupils' writing and note features of spoken language that appear in it, in order to plan ways to help them improve. Become more critical of your own writing. Crystal provides a concise description of the differences between speech and writing in:

Crystal, D. (1996) *Rediscover Grammar*. Longman, pp. 16–19

Another book that looks at this subject, in particular the notion of lexical density, is:

Halliday, M. A. K. (1989) *Spoken and Written Language*. Oxford University Press.

Task E2 – Multilingualism and language variety

Answers
1(d); 2(f); 3(a); 4(c); 5(g); 6(h); 7(e); 8(b).

Feedback
Matching of terms to definitions should have been reasonably straightforward but, in order to understand the implications of knowledge about multilingualism and language variety, the terms defined above (along with some additional terms) are discussed in more detail below.

Accent, dialect and monolingualism

Accent is the way we pronounce words. It can identify a person geographically or socially and can be associated with a particular town or region. Received pronunciation, or RP, is a social accent of English. This accent is not geographically restricted, being found all over Britain and other English-speaking parts of the world. Standard English can be spoken using a variety of accents, amongst which is RP. Examples of regional accents are Cockney and West Country. Regional accents are often attached to dialects of the same name.

Received pronunciation

Standard English is a dialect of English, although it is considered a prestige dialect. Since it, and no other, has the grammar and lexis which is called standard, the other dialects are all labelled non-standard. They each have variations in vocabulary and grammar that make them distinctive. Non-standard use of pronouns and adverbs, and the use of double negatives, are some of the features of non-standard English.

This was examined in the feedback to Task C7.

Accent convergence and divergence

As individuals we may use a variety of accents, depending on our social situation or geographical location at a particular time. During a court appearance, we may use RP; at home in another part of the country, we may use the accent of that geographical region; and away at university or college, we may use another regional accent. This is called 'accent convergence'. If we use one accent in all contexts, we call this 'accent divergence'. Many speakers are also able to move between a non-

There are some famous personalities who are accent divergent; they use their regional or RP accent whatever the context. Which type are you, and have you changed recently?

standard dialect and standard English, so we cannot consider ourselves monolingual, even though we may not speak another language.

Bilingualism, preferred language and first language

Bilingualism

There is a range of bilingual abilities. A neutral definition of bilingualism does not differentiate between greater or lesser fluency, literacy or situational restriction in one language. However, some definitions of bilingualism exclude all but complete fluency in both languages. This leads to a **deficit view** of bilingualism and is therefore to be avoided. Most bilinguals have a **preferred language**, although preferences may vary according to the audience. For example, a bilingual child of parents who have differing first languages may choose to speak one language with each parent, or may choose to speak the same language with both parents, even if the parents use two languages to speak to the child.

Where bilingualism develops with a predominance towards one language, the speaker moves to the dominant language when language is lacking in the other.

Community language and home language

Community and home language

The **community language** of a group may be a standard form of several dialects. For instance, in Asian communities where speakers may be multilingual, Urdu may be used as a community language and a regional dialect may be used as the **home language**.

Common underlying proficiency and linguistic cognates

Common underlying proficiency

One system of thought

For bilinguals, each language involves the use of the same psycho-linguistic processes and serves one central system of thought. A child who has stories read to him in one language will have knowledge about the purpose, structure and messages of narrative that he or she will be able to apply to stories in another language. Similarly, knowledge of topic maintenance and change and turn-taking are transferable from one language to another, although there will be cultural differences between some aspects of language.

Linguistic cognates

In bilingual speakers, **linguistic cognates** are important because new words in one language are understood through their relationships with known words in the other. A richer store of meanings, with the added associations of the second language, is available in the lexicon of a bilingual speaker. Some words have no equivalence in the other language because of the way that the world is semantically divided up, and some words have many more finer distinctions. For example, Arabic has no word for *toes* – the same word is used for *toes* as *fingers*, with toes called *foot fingers* – and the number of Eskimo words for *snow* is legendary. This does not mean that Arabic speakers think of toes differently because of the absence of a specific word, although the way that languages divide up the semantic space that makes our linguistic world has led some linguists to suggest that language determines our way of thinking about it. Hence, Sapir and Whorf's hypothesis of linguistic determinism, which is discussed in Montgomery (1986).

> The political correctness movement and aspects of linguistic engineering lend some support to this theory. Vehicles are now described as pre-owned, rather than second-hand.

Pidgins and creoles

Pidgins and creoles

Pidgins differ from creoles in that, unlike creoles, a pidgin is not the speaker's native language; it is merely developed in order to communicate with others, where speakers do not share a common language. In his book, *The Language Instinct,* Stephen Pinker (1994) discusses creoles in a most enlightening way, pointing out that they are examples of the creation from scratch of complex language rather than a poor attempt at non-native language. He says:

> *Amazingly we can [see how people create a complex language from scratch].*
>
> *The first cases were wrung from two of the more sorrowful episodes of world history, the Atlantic slave trade and indentured servitude in the South Pacific. Perhaps mindful of the Tower of Babel, some of the masters of tobacco, cotton, coffee, and sugar plantations deliberately mixed slaves and labourers from different language backgrounds; others preferred specific ethnicities but had to accept mixtures because that was all that was available. When speakers of different languages have to communicate to carry out practical tasks but do not have the opportunity to learn one another's languages, they develop a make-shift jargon called a pidgin. Pidgins are choppy strings of words borrowed from the language of the colonizers or plantation owners, highly variable in order and with little in the way of grammar. Sometimes a pidgin can become a lingua franca and gradually increase in complexity, as in the 'Pidgin English' of the modern South Pacific. ...*
>
> *But the linguist Derek Bickerton has presented evidence that in many cases a pidgin can be transmuted into a full complex language in one fell swoop: all it takes is for a group of children to be exposed to the pidgin at the age when they acquire their mother tongue. That happened, Bickerton has argued, when children were isolated from their parents and were tended collectively by a worker who spoke to them in the pidgin. Not content to reproduce the fragmentary word strings, the children injected grammatical complexity where none existed before, resulting in a brand-new, richly expressive language. The language that results when children make a pidgin their native tongue is called a creole.* (PP. 32–33)

Pidgin as make-shift language

From pidgin to creole

Child language makes fascinating study. Some references are given in the section on language acquisition in Chapter 3.

Action

Language and identity

Language survey

The importance of language and culture in the construction of identity cannot be underestimated. If you go to a school with a multilingual intake, make a survey of the languages spoken by pupils and staff. In contemporary classrooms pupils need access to texts that reflect their cultures in order to enhance the self-image of bicultural pupils and to broaden the literary experience of the others. West Indian Creole has the status of a heritage language for many black British speakers and is used by poets such as Edward Kamau Brathwaite and Linton Kwesi Johnson.

Make yourself acquainted with a broad range of fiction from world literature and writers who explore the multicultural experience in Britain. See Task G, which lists some multicultural authors.

To extend your knowledge of bilingualism, read Romaine (1989), who has written extensively on the subject. Other useful works include:

Baker, C. (1994) *Foundations of Bilingualism and Bilingual Education.* Multilingual Matters.

Cummins, J. and Swain, M. (1986) *Bilingualism in Education.* Longman.

Task E3 – Historical changes in English

Answers

(a)   Types of linguistic change are:

- Phonological changes in pronunciation. The Great Vowel Shift, between the fourteenth and sixteenth centuries, makes Old English and modern vowels different in many parts of Britain, although the North retains many Old English vowel sounds. For example, the vowel sound in the modern word *oak* would have been pronounced /ɔː/ rather than /oː/ or /əʊ/. Long vowels have tended to change to diphthongs, as in *mouth*, from /uː/ to /aʊ/.

> The Great Vowel Shift is described in Freeborn (1998).

1. Change in orthography. Spelling of Old English words still used in Modern English has changed: sceap (sheep); æx (axe); col (coal); cirice (church).

2. Letter forms and the alphabet used. Old English used the extra vowel æ and consonants: ʒ (now written g); ð, along with a runic letter þ (now replaced by the digraph th), and ρ (now written w). Some consonants were infrequent in Old English: k, q and z, and some not used: j and v.

3. Grammar and word order. The order of clause elements was sometimes different. For example, Freeborn (1998) gives the three examples below. The following labels are used:

   A – adjunct; P – predicator; S – subject; O – object;
   C – complement; cj – conjunction; neg – negative

   (a) After a linking adverb, the verb came before the subject:

      A   P   S   A   A
   then said the serpent after to the woman
   (The Old English is not given here – the sentence is presented word for word in Modern English.)

   (b) The verb might come last in a subordinate clause:

      S   P   A cj S   C   P
   they knew then that they naked were

   (c) Asking questions and forming the negative differed from Modern English:

      A   P   S O cj S neg P
   Why forbade God you that you not eat?

4. Morphology. The system of Old English morphology was far more complex than Modern English. In Modern English nouns inflect only for number (singular and plural) and the possessive case, and verbs in the singular inflect only for the third person. In Old English nouns, verbs and adjectives inflected for each person, gender and case. Freeborn (1998) gives the examples:

> The complex morphological system of Old English is described in Freeborn (1998).

   seo næddre cwæþ   singular feminine nominative
   the   serpent   said

   God cwæþ to þære næddran   singular feminine dative
   God   said   to   the   serpent

Changes in punctuation, vocabulary and meaning

Semantic change

5. Punctuation. Full stops were used both for sentence boundaries and for phrase and clause boundaries where we would use commas and semi-colons today.
6. Vocabulary. Words have been lost, gained and changed in meaning since Old English. Many words are introduced from other languages such as French: *restaurant, café, genre*.
7. Meaning has changed for words that remain in the lexicon since Old English.

(b) Spelling and punctuation have been modernized in this edition of *Julius Caesar*, but we are focusing on form and meaning. Words that are not now used, or that have now changed in form or meaning, are shown in bold and commented on.

Early writing lacked punctuation. Examination of old texts makes us realize that language is not static – it is continually changing.

Look up Old English vocabulary in the wordlist at: http://www.mun.ca/ ansaxdat/vocab/ wordlist.html

ANTONY
*O, pardon me, **thou** bleeding piece of earth,* — Sixteenth-century Early Modern English still used the singular *thou*, rather than *you*.
That I am meek and gentle with these butchers.
*Thou **art** the ruins of the noblest man* — The second person inflection remains.
That ever lived in the tide of times.
Woe to the hand that shed this costly blood!
*Over **thy** wounds now do I prophesy –* — Singular possessive remains.
Which like dumb mouths do ope their ruby lips.
To beg the voice and utterance of my tongue –
A curse shall light upon the limbs of men;
Domestic fury and fierce civil strife
*Shall **cumber** all the parts of Italy;* — Meaning *burden* – (un)encumbered used in Modern English
Blood and destruction shall be so in use,
And dreadful objects so familiar,
That mothers shall but smile when they behold
*Their infants **quartered** with the hands of war,* — Meaning *cut to pieces*
*All pity choked with custom of **fell** deeds;* — Meaning *ruthless* or *terrible*
*And Caesar's spirit, **ranging** for revenge.* — Meaning *seeking*
With Ate by his side, come hot from hell,
Shall in these confines with a monarch's voice
*Cry havoc and **let slip** the dogs of war,* — Meaning *unleash*, as in *give someone the slip* in colloquial Modern English
That this foul deed shall smell above the earth
With carrion men, groaning for burial.
...
***Post** back with speed, and tell him what* — Meaning *travel with haste*
  *hath **chanced**.* — Meaning *happened*
Here is a mourning Rome, a dangerous Rome,
No Rome of safety for Octavius yet.
***Hie hence**, and tell him so. Yet stay awhile;* — Meaning *go away from here*
*Thou shalt not back till I have borne this **corse*** — Meaning *corpse*
*Into the market-place; there shall I **try**,* — Meaning *test*; only used in the legal sense in Modern English
In my oration, how the people take
*The cruel **issue** of these bloody men;* — Meaning *result*
*According to the which, **thou shalt discourse*** — Meaning *talk*; now used only as a noun
To young Octavius of the state of things. — The auxiliary *shalt* inflected for second person singular; auxiliary verbs no longer inflect.
Lend me your hand.

(III.I. LINES 255–297)

Feedback

If you have studied Old and Middle English and the history of the language, this section will be very familiar to you. If, however, you did not study these areas on your degree course, much of this will be unfamiliar. The study of changes in vocabulary, meaning and word order are important in the study of literature. For example, meanings of words have changed since Chaucer or Shakespeare, and some words have disappeared from use or changed in meaning. From the extract above, we can see that some senses of a word have dropped out of usage, or are only used in specialized contexts today, for example, *try* and *discourse* (as a verb).

Action

Freeborn's book, looking at changes in English from Old English to Modern standard English, is a good reference work:

> Freeborn, D. (1998) *From Old English to Standard English.* Macmillan.

To investigate changes in word meaning, use, spelling and punctuation, look for unmodernized texts and use them in conjunction with a modernized version and the *Oxford English Dictionary,* which gives etymology and lists changes. To investigate changes of meaning, look up the words *pretty* and *buxom* and see how meaning has changed between Old and Modern English.

Etymology and the dictionary

Section F:

Knowledge about texts and critical approaches to them

Response to text

Task F1 – Response to fiction and non-fiction

Answers

You will probably have found this task rather subjective. In fact, all the skills listed are found in the reading section of the National Curriculum, demonstrating the arbitrariness of the categorization of skills. The table below and on the following page summarizes the National Curriculum skills for reading, and speaking and listening, that are involved in response to text.

National Curriculum skills

THE NATIONAL CURRICULUM AND RESPONSE TO TEXT	
SPEAKING AND LISTENING	**READING**
• use talk to explore ideas and hypothesize	• extract meaning beyond the literal through explanation of language and style
• use talk for the purpose of considering ideas	• extract implicit and hidden meanings as well as explicit ones
• use talk for the development of thinking	• analyse alternative interpretations; recognize ambiguity
• listen attentively	• analyse and engage with the ideas themes and language
• in discussions, take different views into account, sift, summarize, use salient points, cite evidence and construct persuasive arguments	• reflect on the impact of the text through the presentation of ideas, characters and plot
	• distinguish between attitudes of the author and those displayed by the characters
	• appreciate the characteristics of high quality literature
• articulate informed personal opinions (in reading attainment)	• appreciate the significance of Biblical, mythological and intertextual allusions and references
	• consider how texts are changed when adapted to different media

These skills are summarized from the National Curriculum.

THE NATIONAL CURRICULUM AND RESPONSE TO TEXT *(CONTINUED)*	
SPEAKING AND LISTENING	**READING**
• discuss alternative interpretations (in reading attainment)	• select relevant information and evidence objectively, distinguishing between fact and opinion, and make effective use of it • compare and synthesize information drawn from different sources

Feedback

In your response to the task you will have demonstrated how arbitrary the division of skills is. Many of the skills can be developed equally well both through talk and reading and in pupils' writing. What is important is the consideration and selection of appropriate texts and extracts when developing reading, writing, and speaking and listening skills. Sometimes a whole text will be used and at other times short extracts for close analysis and discussion. We should never forget the importance of fostering enjoyment and enthusiasm for text, and when introducing Shakespeare, for example, the careful selection of passages and events, rather than detailed reading of the entire text, will support the development of a positive and receptive response from pupils.

With non-fiction, the use of DARTS activities (Directed Activities Related to Texts) is beneficial. These include cloze procedure, transforming texts from one genre to another, comprehension activities, diagrammatic representations and reconstructions of cut-up texts.

Action

Some useful readings and suggestions for developing response are:

> Abbs, P. and Richardson, J. (1990) *The Forms of Narrative: A Practical Study Guide for English*. Cambridge University Press. (Consists of an anthology of extracts, with ideas for development and follow-up with each extract.)

> Davison, J. and Dowson, J. (1998) *Learning to Teach English in the Secondary School*, (Chapter 6). Routledge.

> Protherough, R. (1983) *Developing Response to Fiction*. Open University Press.

> Protherough, R. (1995) 'What is a Reading Curriculum?' in R. Protherough and P. King, *The Challenge of English in the National Curriculum*, pp.30–47. Routledge.

> Thomson, J. (1987) *Understanding Teenagers' Reading: Reading Processes and the Teaching of Literature*. Methuen Australia. (A developmental model of reader-response in teenagers' reading of fiction.)

Task F2 – Presentation of information and ideas

Answers

(a)   The seven examples are matched to the six text types in the table on the facing page.

Sidebar notes:

Enjoyment and enthusiasm for text

DARTS activities as response to non-fiction

See Davison and Dowson (1998) for more on DARTS activities.

Wray, D. and Lewis, M. (1997) has useful practical suggestions and knowledge for younger pupils.

	TEXT TYPE	EFFECT OF CONTEXT ON PRESENTATION OF INFORMATION AND IDEAS	TEXT(S)
Text type and the presentation of ideas	A	ideas of cause and effect are logically connected and good and evil are presented in clearly defined characters; the issue of obedience to parents is reinforced whilst also being presented in an entertaining story, which creates suspense, evil and resolution of evil; use of illustration.	*Little Red Riding Hood*
	B	the effect is a discursive, informal style with a sometimes conspiratorial, sometimes sarcastic tone.	A feature article in a teenage magazine for girls.
	C	uses effects such as humour, self-endorsement, identification; plays on viewer's ideal self image.	A television advertisement for an alcoholic drink.
	D	the reader is given many viewpoints; the author explores (and makes the reader explore) the positions of each of the characters, making this a psychological exploration of character and interaction.	Jean Rhys's *Wide Sargasso Sea*.
	E	a step-by-step procedure is given to be followed; use of instructions for action and use of diagrams to support text and illustrate location of parts.	A recipe. A section in a Haynes's car manual, outlining the procedure for inspecting and renewing the rear brake linings on a car.
	F	ideas presented clearly, graphically, concisely, informatively and educationally; technical terms explained and defined.	BBC Television's *Newsround*.

Tense and narrative

(b) A range of tenses is used for the narration at the end of the novel. The three emboldened sections are commented on below.

1. The extract starts in the past tense (*was*) and moves in the second sentence into the present (*know*) and then the present progressive (*watching*). This use of the present tense makes the event immediate.

2. The narrated dream is in the past tense, told as a recollection that is also being reflected upon. Occasionally there is a present tense comment, as in *They think I don't remember, but I do.*

3. In the final paragraph the narration moves from the past back to the present tense and then finishes in the past, the reader realizing at this point that the narration is from beyond the grave.

Change of viewpoint

The narration is often confusing for readers because of this time shifting and change of viewpoint. One has to question whether the narrator is living or ghostly and at the same time perceive the movements in present and past time. In this extract, the present tense sentences move the narrator from being awake in bed to outside the bedroom after some time on the same night. The past tense narration moves between a point after all the action has ended, to the recent past from a particular point in time of the story, and at the end back to the point after all the action is ended.

Feedback
The tasks in this section are intended to raise your awareness of the ways in which texts present information. Knowledge about how information and ideas are presented is central to the interpretation of text.

Genre was also discussed in the feedback to Task D2.

Genre and the presentation of information and ideas

Genre affects the presentation of information and ideas because, in the process of writing, we create generic products:

- narratives – use techniques of narration through the process of sequencing events and setting characters in terms of place and time

- essays, reviews and persuasive texts – use techniques of argument through the process of persuasion and careful, logical ordering of points

- procedural texts such as science reports – use techniques of communication that instruct and explain through description of a sequence of events or instructions

- information texts such as descriptions, reports and definitions – use techniques that describe and classify

Connected with genre are the kinds of presentational devices linked to the writer, the context and the intended audience and purpose of the text. The table below lists the contextual features of the six texts featured in the task. By comparing the texts, you can see the similarities and differences between some of the texts and their features.

Contextual features of texts

CONTEXTUAL FEATURES OF TEXTS			
TEXT	WRITER'S POINT OF VIEW	AUDIENCE CONSIDERATIONS	PURPOSE(S) OF THE TEXT
A: *Little Red Riding Hood*	moralistic; teaching	uses familiar language and structure and repetition to keep interest and intrigue	to entertain with a moral
B: article in girls' magazine	social informer; wise youthful aunt; gossip	age, experience and concerns taken into account	to provide social information, reduce anxiety, empathize
C: TV advert	encouraging drinking partner	identifies with habits, aspirations and desires	to persuade, create desire and sell
D: *Wide Sargasso Sea*	first person narration, but from the point of view of several of the characters	involves the audience in considering a story from several perspectives	to evoke understanding and empathy for the characters
E: Haynes's car manual	instructional; expert to lesser expert	step-by-step instructions, but assumes a prior level of some considerable skill	to explain a procedure and provide instructions to complete a job
F: BBC TV's *Newsround*	adult to child; instructional as well as informative	explains and informs using accessible language and formats; low level of prior knowledge assumed	to explain, educate and inform

Narrator

Narrative has its own generic features. One of the distinctive features is the author's choice of voice. Some different types of narrator are:

- first-person narrator
- third-person narrator
- omniscient narrator
- 'fallible' narrator
- self-conscious narrator who produces a reflexive work

- narrator as character
- author as narrator
- a mixture of narrators
- narrator changes

Authorial techniques

There are many other presentational and authorial techniques open to writers of fiction and non-fiction. Here is a selection:

- parallel narratives
- use of setting
- use of period
- story within a story
- time shifts
- use of letters
- use of themes
- use of a feminist, moralist or satirical perspective

- building of suspense
- use of imagery
- plot and structure
- use of genre
- use of fact and opinion
- use of bias and objectivity
- use of the relevant and irrelevant

Action
Continue to develop the level of observation and analysis begun here by collecting or making notes on a wide range of texts from fiction, non-fiction and the media.

F3 – Implication, undertone, bias, assertion and ambiguity

Answers
The variety of possible responses here makes it impossible to give definitive answers. What is important is that you have looked up any terms you are not clear about, and looked closely at text in a way that will help you establish a repertoire of examples that you can build on and use with pupils.

Feedback

Tone

Implication, undertone, bias, assertion and ambiguity can all be described as being aspects of the tone of a text. In speech, this is often evident in the intonation, gesture and body language of the speaker. In writing, it is more difficult to identify how the writer is positioning him or herself in relation to what they are saying. Readers have to use their judgement. Judgement involves locating the sources of evidence that point to the writer's position.

Judgement and evidence

Writers may be explicit in their assertions, or may involve readers in searching and coming to their own conclusions using implicit or well-hidden clues.

The speaking and listening component of the National Curriculum outlines some of the judgements listeners need to be taught to make in relation to the implications of speech. These are equally applicable to pupils' judgements about writing, in terms both of being able to locate indicators of intention in the work of professional writers and using them appropriately, with effect, in their own writing:

National Curriculum skills

> *In order to develop as effective listeners, pupils should be taught to identify the major elements of what is being said, and to distinguish tone, undertone, implications and other indicators of the speaker's intentions. They should be taught to notice ambiguities, deliberate vagueness, glossing over points, use and abuse of evidence, and unsubstantiated statements.* (P. 18)

Media

Critical approaches

Action

The task merely asks you to look at three of the terms. Extend your knowledge by considering the remaining terms in relation to examples from texts you know well and new texts.

Extend your coverage of examples to other media, including film, television programmes, magazines, newspapers and other non-fiction texts. Look for ways of comparing tone in speech and writing. Consider the importance of intonation in reading text aloud and the effect on the tone and implication of a text read with varied stress, intonation and emphasis.

Text F4 – Critical approaches

Answers

(a)   (a)4; (b)8; (c)2; (d)1; (e)5; (f)7; (g)6; (h)3.

(b)   Suggested approaches are shown for each of the texts.

TEXT	APPROACH(ES)
Animal Farm	Marxist or Biographical
Jane Eyre	Psycho-analytical, Feminist, Marxist
The French Lieutenant's Woman	Post-structuralist, Reader-response
The Color Purple	Psycho-analytical, Feminist, Biographical
The Name of the Rose	Reader-response
Brighton Rock	Psycho-analytical
Little Red Riding Hood	Structuralist, Feminist
The poetry of Dylan Thomas	Stylistic
The Turbulent Term of Tyke Tyler	Feminist, Reader-response

> Why might these approaches be useful with these particular texts?

Feedback

(a)   These are very short definitions of literary theories, which are expanded and explained in any good book on literary theory. Entire books are devoted to many of these. Some of the techniques used by each approach and the ways in which each focuses on reading are shown in the table below and on the facing page.

CRITICAL APPROACHES		
APPROACH	**TECHNIQUES**	**WAYS OF READING**
Reader-response theory	examines clues and signs in the characterization and textualization and their implications; collects patterns and intra-textual strings of references and associations; collects recurring images, metaphors and themes; focuses on language and oppositions.	involves the reader in being an active constructor and interpreter of meaning; involves an open, reflective and inquisitive approach to reading and meaning.
Feminist criticism	examines stereotypes and positions of oppression and inequality for women; examines characterization and ideology in the text; examines struggles of power and oppression, freedom and constraint.	involves the reader in analysis of gender stereotypes and his or her own position in relation to the characters and their experiences; involves consciousness raising.

Techniques and ways
of reading

CRITICAL APPROACHES *(CONTINUED)*		
APPROACH	**TECHNIQUES**	**WAYS OF READING**
Biographical criticism	examines particular events in the biography of the author and the influences on text production and product; compares events recounted in the autobiography of an author with similar events in their novels.	involves the reader in the analysis of events from both the perspective of the author's biography and the way similar events are characterized and narrated.
Marxist criticism	examines the social positions of the characters and their reactions to their state; uncovers the existing and sometimes conflicting ideologies inherent in the text and how these determine the behaviour and construction of the characters.	the ideological, political and social positions that the reader brings to the text influence the reading; a Marxist reading in itself may be as a result of the position of the reader in relation to the text.
Structuralism	examines the structural and linguistic systems in texts, particularly in terms of the way language signifies and creates associations; uses Saussure's distinction between *langue* and *parole*; examines narrative in terms of its structures and oppositions.	involves the reader in the process of active construction of meaning; involves the reader in constructing the author's message.
Psycho-analytical criticism	examines relationships between characters: mother and son, adult and child, repressions, obsessions and compulsions; examines childhood experiences and their influence on adult behaviour; uses Freudian imagery and interpretation of dreams in the process of interpretation.	involves analysis of the characters in terms of their Freudian associations, such as relationships between mother and son and adult and child; involves interpretation of the text through Freudian imagery.
Post-structuralism	examines the multiple and alternative meanings of texts by a process of deconstruction that involves looking for gaps and contradictions in the narrative; examines the figurative language, associations and allusions in the text.	the reader is a powerful central focus of the text, having freedom to deconstruct meaning; in contrast to a structuralist reading, the status of the author is not one of power and influence, but of enabler and questioner.
Stylistics	examines a text objectively and sometimes statistically in terms of the grammar, lexis, rhetoric, semantics, meter or phonology; analyses the contribution of textual features to meaning and effect.	involves the reader in collecting, ordering and analysing examples of stylistic features; statistical and manual collection of examples is done after reading, following impressions gained while reading – objective judgements follow subjective ones.

Pupils should be introduced to a range of ways of reading in order to evaluate and respond to text.

The contents of the table are not to be considered as a finite list of techniques or ways of reading. You will be able to think of others and can add to those listed here in the course of time.

Approaches to text

It should be remembered that readings and approaches to texts are often influenced by the positions of readers themselves in relation to texts. One could argue that a Marxist reading of a nineteenth-century novel from a twentieth-century perspective will result in a particular bias that would not have been available to the intended readers. However, in studying literature, one cannot argue against the contribution of diverse readings to the effect and meaning of a work for the reader. All contributions to interpretation should be considered and evaluated.

Diverse readings and interpretation

(b)   This is not an absolute list and, where an approach is suggested, it is more important that you consider why the use of that approach may be beneficial to the interpretation of the text. With your own examples, you will have considered this.

Action

(a)   Some useful books on critical theory for teachers of English are:

Burton, M. (ed.) (1989) *Enjoying Texts: Using Literary Theory in the Classroom*. Stanley Thornes.

Peim, N. (1993) *Critical Theory and the English Teacher*. Routledge.

As a student English teacher, you will probably never read a text again without considering how you might use it or introduce it to pupils of a particular age or ability. Make notes, as you read new texts, on techniques or ways of reading that could be applied to them in order to develop interpretive judgement.

(b)   In your familiarization with a broad range of texts (suggested in response to Task G) consider approaches to individual texts that will enhance interpretation and produce questioning readings rather than a predominance of readings that search for the 'truth' or the definitive meaning.

Section G:

Knowledge of a range of texts

Research

Task G – Authors and texts

Answers

(a)   No answers are given for this section. The intention is to involve you in some research in your university, college, or school's library and its catalogue, to check and develop your knowledge.

(b)   The 'real' authors of children's literature are separated from the others in the table that follows.

Children's literature

CHILDREN'S LITERATURE		
AUTHORS OF CHILDREN'S LITERATURE		**OTHER AUTHORS**
Nina Bawden Betsy Byars Lewis Carroll Helen Cresswell Gillian Cross Anne Fine Leon Garfield Alan Garner Ursula Le Guin Judith Kerr Gene Kemp Clive King	Dick King-Smith C. S. Lewis Jack London Jenny Nimmo Robert O'Brien Terry Pratchett Rosemary Sutcliff John Rowe Townsend E. B. White Jacqueline Wilson Paul Zindel	John Austin Margaret Berry Margaret Clark Bruce Fraser John Gibbons Robert Kaplan Judith Levi Jim Martin Wendy Morgan Michael Stubbs Henry Widdowson

(c)   Details of book awards and one or more titles given the award are shown below.

Children's book awards

CHILDREN'S BOOK AWARDS		
AWARD	**GIVEN FOR AND BY ...**	**AUTHORS, TITLES AND DATE OF AWARD**
Carnegie Medal	a children's book of outstanding merit, by the British Library Association.	Mary Norton *The Borrowers* (1952) Phillippa Pearce *Tom's Midnight Garden* (1958)
Kate Greenaway Medal	the most distinguished work in the illustration of children's books, by the British Library Association.	Janet Ahlberg *Each Peach Pear Plum* (1978) Charles Keeping *The Highwayman* (1981)
Guardian Award	children's (and adult) fiction, by the *Guardian* newspaper.	Michelle Magorian *Goodnight Mr Tom* (1982) Richard Adams *Watership Down* (1973)
Smarties Prize	for works for children aged 9–11 years, 6–8 years and 5 years and under.	Joanne Rowling *Harry Potter and the Philosopher's Stone* (1997) Pauline Fisk *Midnight Blue* (1990)
The Whitbread Awards	for popular appeal and wide readability, by the brewers of the same name.	Andrew Noriss *Aquila* (1997) Anne Fine *The Tulip Touch* (1996)

> All this information (and more) can be found on literary award websites on the Internet.

Adult book awards

ADULT BOOK AWARDS		
AWARD	**GIVEN FOR AND BY ...**	**AUTHORS, TITLES AND DATE OF AWARD**
The Booker Prize	fiction in English, by a panel of well-known judges.	Anita Brookner *Hotel du Lac* (1984) Penelope Lively *Moon Tiger* (1987)
The Nobel Prize for Literature	the most outstanding work of an idealistic tendency, under the terms of the will of Alfred Nobel.	Rudyard Kipling (1907) Ernest Hemingway (1954) John Steinbeck (1962) Wole Soyinka (1986)
The Whitbread Awards	novel, first novel, biography, children's novel and poetry, by the brewers of the same name.	1997 AWARDS novel: Jim Crace *Quarantine* first novel: Pauline Melville *The Ventriloquist's Tale* poetry: Ted Hughes *Tales from Ovid* biography: Graham Robb *Victor Hugo*

ADULT BOOK AWARDS (continued)		
AWARD	**GIVEN FOR AND BY …**	**AUTHORS, TITLES AND DATE OF AWARD**
The Somerset Maugham Prize	writers under 35, by The Society of Authors.	A. L. Kennedy *Looking for the Possible Dance* (1993)
Prix Goncourt	the best imaginative prose work, preferably a novel, by the Académie Goncourt.	Andreï Makine *Le Testament Français* (1996)
The Pulitzer Prize	'the American novel which shall best present the wholesome atmosphere of American life, and the highest standards of American manners and manhood', under Josef Pulitzer's will.	John Steinbeck *The Grapes of Wrath* (1940)

Look up a complete list of prize winners and some texts on the Pulitzer Prize Archive on the Internet.

Breadth of knowledge

Action

Evaluate your knowledge of texts and identify areas where breadth of knowledge is poor. Target books and authors and text-types for reading (including CD-ROMs and Internet sites) and keep a log of your reading and some kind of review of books, providing you with a record of key information, such as summary of plot, themes, characters, accompanying resources (such as video and audio tapes, CD-ROMs, handbooks and guides) and practical uses for the classroom that you have tried and observed.

There are many more children's and adult book awards:

> The Children's Book Award
> Emil (Kurt Maschler) Award
> Mother Goose Award

as well as other British, American, French and Italian major book awards. Some of these are described in:

> Cuddon, J. A. (1992) *The Penguin Dictionary of Literary Terms and Literary Theory* (third edition). Penguin (See 'literary prizes'.)

> Sawyer, W., Watson, K. and Adams, A. (eds.) (1989) *English Teaching from A-Z*. Open University Press. (Titles, authors and dates of awards are given.)

Internet websites

Reviews

Details of children's and adult book awards can be found at Internet websites. Exchange reviews with fellow students and compile a list of useful Internet sites found. In addition, investigate the range of multicultural fiction written specifically for children and secondary pupils. Carol MacDougall, in Lee (1987), discusses the role of multicultural literature and gives a book list that would serve as a good starting point from which to build, with recently published novels, short stories, myths, folk tales and poetry.

A level, GCSE and Key Stage 3 texts

Familiarize yourself with the approved texts for A level syllabuses and the texts for GCSE and Key Stage 3 tests.

Collect non-fiction texts – advertisements, articles, letters, reports and documents – from a range of media, including newspapers, magazines, television, film, radio and ephemera, for use with pupils.

Developing your knowledge

Introduction

Where are you now?

The question *What is English Subject Knowledge?* was asked in the audit introduction. When you thought about this, you may well have been very clear about your answer. On carrying out the audit and evaluating your knowledge in terms of the requirements of the ITTNC, you may now have a different response to that question.

The nature of English subject knowledge is such that its breadth and scope are very wide. English is not only a subject covering a wide number of sub-disciplines, it is also one that serves all the other curriculum areas through teaching the skills of reading, writing, speaking and listening. Knowledge related to literature, non-fiction and linguistics is therefore only part of the picture; the knowledge related to punctuation, spelling, grammar, genre and structure, called the lexical, grammatical and textual skills of literacy, is also essential. In addition, the technical metalanguage needed to analyse, discuss, teach and read research on these skills must be familiar to you. As prospective English teachers, then, you will be responsible for developing literacy in addition to both the areas of literary and linguistic knowledge.

In a book of this length, it is impossible to develop all the sub-disciplines of English raised in the audit and by the National Curriculum and examination syllabuses for English language and literature. Each section of the feedback therefore:

- develops the subject knowledge focused on in the tasks covered in the audit
- then suggests ways to develop that knowledge further in the action

However, the tasks are merely samples of knowledge, raised for the purposes of the audit. There are many aspects of knowledge that could have been focused on and are not; the knowledge audited here is therefore selective. There is some bias towards linguistic knowledge, since literary knowledge is likely to be more common to your experience.

Bearing all these things in mind, we now need to consider where development is needed and how to go about it.

Literature, linguistics and literacy

What do I do next?

There are a number of things that you could do now:

1. From your marking of the audit, you should have been able to **identify your areas of strength and weakness**. Make a record of these. You may have been asked to record this information in a profile that will lead to assessment at the end of your course and be recorded in your Career Entry Profile.

Follow the steps outlined in the *Personal Learning Plan* at the end of this book.

2. After reading the feedback to each task, you should have been able to assess whether your knowledge is secure or not. The action suggested to follow up each task will develop knowledge in areas where it is less secure. **Follow this action, or set yourself your own individual targets**, again making a record of what you are planning to develop through personal study and your taught course. This may involve reading, talking to experienced teachers, observing and questioning children, and planning, teaching and evaluating a lesson that focuses on the learning of a selected aspect of knowledge.

3. **Make yourself an action plan or checklist** of priority areas for development and areas for extension and consolidation.

4. **Check off items as you cover them** through your course, in school, or through self-study, noting what you have done.

5. You may **re-audit your knowledge** at a later point in your course and towards the end, in order **to check progress**.

6. **Seek help** if you need it. Tutors, teachers in school and fellow students are all useful sources of help. Peer study-groups can be very helpful.

Defining and developing knowledge

To help you move on and develop your knowledge, it might be helpful to clarify the knowledge to which we are referring. Pages 98–101 of Section C of the ITTNC set out 'Trainees' knowledge and understanding of English'. This knowledge complements the pedagogical knowledge and teaching and assessment methods outlined in Sections A and B. The audit in this book has been written in direct response to Section C of the ITTNC. Paragraph 29 of this section sets out additional knowledge for post-16 literary and linguistic study. Whilst the knowledge required is contained in the audit, the depth of knowledge required cannot solely be audited through the kind of tasks used here. Essays or assignments as a result of detailed study will be more appropriate for auditing this.

It is useful, however, to consider the areas that should be covered, and incorporate these into the complete picture of English as a discipline. The diagram below shows this picture of literary and linguistic knowledge, surrounded by the knowledge of literacy and resources that serves them. This chapter concludes with a summary of the key knowledge in each area, with additional reading.

Defining knowledge

Literacy knowledge
punctuation • spelling • grammar • paragraphing
genre and structure • presentational knowledge • word processing

Literary knowledge
• knowledge of a range of texts and authors from different periods
• the three main genres: poetry, fiction and drama
• knowledge of a variety of forms: sonnet, ballad
• a range of critical approaches and appreciation

stylistics

Linguistic knowledge
• phonology and phonetics
• semantics and lexis
• sociolinguistics
• grammar
• language change
• language acquisition

Knowledge of resources
CD-ROM • use of ICT • media, film and non-fiction texts • Internet

Literary knowledge

Texts and authors

A range of texts and authors

Breadth of knowledge is essential. Task G illustrates this range. Useful reference works are the various companions to literature:

Berney, K. A. (ed.) (1994) *Contemporary British Dramatists*. St. James Press.

Blain, V., Clements, P. and Grundy, I. (eds.) (1990) *The Feminist Companion to Literature in English*. B. T. Batsford Ltd.

Chevalier, Y. (ed.) (1993) *Contemporary World Writers*. St. James Press.

Davidson, C. and Wagner-Martin, L. (eds.) (1995) *The Oxford Companion to Women's Writing in the United States*. Oxford University Press.

Drabble, M. (ed.) (1985) *The Oxford Companion to Literature in English*. Oxford University Press.

Hart, J. D. (1986) *The Concise Oxford Companion to American Literature*. Oxford University Press.

Ousby, I. (ed.) (1988) *The Cambridge Guide to Literature in English*. Cambridge University Press.

Shattock, J. (1993) *The Oxford Guide to British Women Writers*. Oxford University Press.

Thieme, J. (1996) *The Arnold Anthology of Post-Colonial Literatures in English*. Arnold.

Poetry, fiction and drama

The three main genres

Knowledge of each genre – poetry, fiction and drama – is important in literary studies. Within each genre, there are in addition the sub-genres. Cuddon (1992) lists the major classical genres: epic, tragedy, lyric, comedy and satire. We label sub-genres with names such as rap, nonsense verse, detective fiction, fantasy fiction, journal, diary, short story, farce, theatre of the absurd, soap opera. Task G gives some broad generic headings, but a greater depth of knowledge of the sub-genres is important. The development of a literature file containing reviews and suggestions for teaching would be extremely valuable.

Form and genre

Literary forms

Form and genre are almost interchangeable and are sometimes used synonymously. It is worth making a distinction, however. We could say that each genre consists of different forms of writing. We would talk about dramatic monologue as a form rather than a genre – unless a whole text consisted of dramatic monologue. Performers and writers such as Maureen Lipman and Alan Bennett use this particular genre. Other literary forms are first- and third-person narrative, dialogue, use of letters, story within a story, allegory, verse and stanza, blank verse, prologue, soliloquy. Form is therefore an element of genre.

Useful texts

Abbs, P. and Richardson, J. (1990) *The Forms of Narrative*. Cambridge University Press (with a companion: *The Forms of Poetry*).

Criticism and appreciation

Critical approaches and appreciation

Theories and approaches to criticism include Bakhtinian criticism, feminist criticism, Marxist criticism, modernism, post-structuralism, psychoanalytical criticism, reader-reception theory, and structuralism. Appreciation involves response to literature and stimulates the imagination and creativity. Knowledge of literary figures includes allusion, extended metaphor, metaphor, simile and symbol.

Useful texts

Cuddon, J. A. (1992) *The Penguin Dictionary of Literary Terms and Literary Theory* (third edition). Penguin.
Green, K. and LeBihan, J. (eds.) (1996) *Critical Theory and Practice: A Coursebook*. Routledge.
Lodge, D. (1988) *Modern Criticism and Theory: A Reader*. Longman.
The journal: *Theory into Practice*. Ohio State University.

Linguistic knowledge

Introductions to linguistics

If you have not studied linguistics in any detail, the following texts provide a useful introduction:

Crystal, D. (1995) *The Cambridge Encyclopaedia of the English Language*. Cambridge University Press.
Graddol, D., Cheshire, J. and Swann, J. (1994) *Describing Language* (second edition). Open University Press.
Kuiper, K. and Scott Allan, W. (1996) *An Introduction to English Language*. Macmillan.
Malmkjaer, K. (ed.) (1991) *The Linguistics Encyclopedia*. Routledge.
Pinker, S. (1994) *The Language Instinct*. Penguin.
Robins, R. H. (1989) *General Linguistics: An Introductory Survey* (fourth edition). Longman.

Stylistics and objectivity

Stylistics

Stylistics aims to objectify the study of literature through analysis of the lexical and grammatical choices made by an author. It therefore straddles the literary and linguistic disciplines, using knowledge of lexis, word order and grammar to help make objective judgements about a writer's style. Aspects of style can then be collected in order to describe the features characteristic of a particular writer or text. Stylistic features are different from generic features. Generic features are structural components common to a body of texts and come about because of the identical purpose of those texts, although they may be characterized by particular phrases or vocabulary. Stylistic features relate more closely to content and individual choice rather than structural features.

Useful texts

Carter, R. (ed.) (1982) *Language and Literature*. Allen & Unwin.
Fowler, R. (1986) *Linguistic Criticism*. Oxford University Press.
Freeborn, D. (1996) *Style*. Macmillan.
Leech, G. (1969) *A Linguistic Guide to English Poetry*. Longman.

Grammar and morphology

Descriptive grammars

Descriptive grammars, such as Halliday's (1985) systemic-functional grammar, Quirk et al. (1985), Sinclair (1990) and Greenbaum (1990), describe the grammatical features of language. Grammatical knowledge is used in the study of reading, writing and speech, from stylistics to the study of dialect. Also included in grammar is the study of morphology in the inflection of verbs and nouns. Knowledge of grammar includes knowledge of the system of grammar and the usage of that system in reading, writing and speech.

Useful texts

Greenbaum, S. (1990) *The Oxford English Grammar*. Oxford University Press.
Halliday, M. A. K. (1985) *An Introduction to Functional Grammar*. Arnold.
QCA (1998) *The Grammar Papers. Perspectives on the Teaching of Grammar in the National Curriculum*. QCA (Qualifications and Curriculum Authority).
Quirk, R., Greenbaum, S., Leech, G. N. and Svartvik, J. A. (1985) *A Comprehensive Grammar of the English Language*. Longman.
Sinclair, J. (ed.) (1990) *Collins COBUILD English Grammar*. Collins ELT.

> This is a very recent re-examination of grammar in schools.

Sociolinguistics

Language and society

Sociolinguistics covers areas of linguistics that relate to society's use of language: accent and dialect, gender and power, pidgins and creoles, bilingualism, language variety, and English as a world language.

Useful texts

Fairclough, N. (1989) *Language and Power*. Longman.
Freeborn, D. (1986) *Varieties of English* (second edition). Macmillan.
Holmes, J. (1992) *An Introduction to Sociolinguistics*. Longman.
Hughes, A. and Trudgill, P. (1979) *English Accents and Dialects*. Arnold.
Montgomery, M. (1986) *An Introduction to Language and Society*. Methuen.
Romaine, S. (1989) *Bilingualism*. Blackwell.
Trudgill, P. (1983) *Sociolinguistics: An Introduction to Language and Society* (revised edition). Penguin.

Wardhaugh, R. (1986) *An Introduction to Sociolinguistics.*
Blackwell.

Historical change

Language change

The study of how the English language has evolved and changed involves looking at the variety of linguistic influences and the changes that have taken place in word order, spelling, morphology, meaning, usage, phonology and alphabet. English has a long written history and wide influences and borrowings from other languages that account for the many changes in orthography.

Useful text

Freeborn, D. (1998) *From Old English to Standard English.* Macmillan (This text gives other useful references.)

Language acquisition

Language acquisition

Language acquisition involves the study of how children acquire language. Other areas of linguistics are needed to describe the development of phonology, lexis, semantics, grammar, morphology, body language and discourse structures.

Useful texts

Fletcher, P. and Garman, M. (1979) *Language Acquisition.* Cambridge University Press.
Foster, S. H. (1990) *The Communicative Competence of Young Children.* Longman.
Peccei, J. Stilwell (1995) *Child Language.* Routledge.

Lexis and semantics

Lexis and semantics

Knowledge of the lexicon, words, their meanings and semantic relationships between them is important to the study of text. Knowledge is important in stylistics, language acquisition, language change and the study of literary and non-literary texts.

Useful texts

Aitchison, J. (1987) *Words in the Mind: An Introduction to the Mental Lexicon.* Blackwell.
Carter, R. (1987) *Vocabulary.* Allen & Unwin.
Leech, G. (1981) *Semantics* (second edition). Penguin.

Phonology and phonetics

Phonology and phonetics

Phonology is the study of the sound and intonation of language and is centred on the study of phonemes. Phonetics involves the study of speech sounds, their production and articulation. Sound and letter correspondences are important to the learning of reading and spelling. In English pronounced with Received Pronunciation there are around 44 individual sounds. Regional variation adds to this number. We can sub-classify these sounds into vowel and consonant phonemes, since words are made by combining consonant and vowel sounds (CVC – cat; CVCV – water). There are 20 vowel phonemes and 24 consonant phonemes represented by the symbols of the International Phonetic

There will be weak readers in Key Stage 3 who need to develop their phonic knowledge. This is also an important strategy for spelling.

IPA

Alphabet (IPA). These are listed in the table below, with examples of words containing the sounds. The variety of graphemes that represent the sounds is also shown.

VOWEL PHONEMES	EXAMPLES	GRAPHEMES
SHORT VOWELS		
/ɪ/	ship, myth, build, manage	i y ui a
/ʊ/	book, bush, would, woman	oo u ou o
/e/	jet, head	e ea
/æ/	cat, active	a
/ʌ/	cup, some, country	u o ou
/ɒ/	hot, quality, because	o a au
/ə/	sofa, about, obey, other, forward, circumference, comfort, company, famous	a o ar ir e or ou
LONG VOWELS		
/iː/	bee, even, mean, believe, receive, police, these	ee e ea ie ei i
/aː/	father, hearth, harm, palm	a ear ar al
/ɔː/	paw, order, audible, awful, bought, more, roar, door, your	aw or au ou ore oar oor our
/uː/	moon, group, Ruth, move, too, dew, Jew	oo ou u o e
/ɜː/	bird, early, person, burn, curb, occur, journey worst, first	ir ear er ur our or
DIPHTHONGS		
/eɪ/	ray	ay
/aɪ/	pie, fly, right, guide, alibi, time	ie y i ui
/ɔɪ/	toy, toil, royal	oy oi
/əʊ/	phone, moan, soul, bowl, toe	o oa ou o oe
/aʊ/	how, snout, mound, town	ow ou
/ɪə/	here, ear, pier, beer, weir	ere ear ier eer eir
/eə/	fair, parent, ware, bear, there	ai a are ear ere
/ʊə/	sure, tour	ure our
UNVOICED CONSONANTS		
/b/	boy, rubber	b bb
/k/	kill, lick, car, chord	k ck c ch
/d/	dog, rudder	d dd
/g/	go, bigger, ghost	g gg gh
/h/	hill, whole	h wh
/dʒ/	jug, generate, bridge, large	j g dg ge
/l/	letter, hill	l ll
/m/	mother, bomb, column, summer	m mb mn mm
/tʃ/	chew, catch, question	ch tch ti
/p/	pig, apple	p pp
/r/	rug, horror, rhinoceros, write	r rr rh wr
/t/	tin, bitter, walked, pterodactyl	t tt ed pt
/w/	water, which, persuade	w wh u
/y/	yes	y
/n/	no, sign, gnat, knife, tanner	n gn kn nn
/ŋ/	ring	ng
PAIRS OF UNVOICED AND VOICED CONSONANTS		
/s/	song, psalm, scene, disciple, listen, cross	s ps sc st ss
/z/	zoo, dogs, dizzy, maze	z s zz
/ʃ/	shoe, chef, schedule, sugar, fission, mention, crucial, machine	sh ch sch s ssi ti ci
/ʒ/	fusion, regime, barrage, measure	si g s
/f/	fat, offer, phone, laugh, life	f ff ph gh
/v/	van	v
/θ/	thing, breath	th
/ð/	this, breathe	th

Short vowels

The short vowel sound /æ/ has the closest graphic correspondence.

Long vowels

Some sounds, such as /ɔː/ and /ɜː/, have as many as nine different graphic forms.

Diphthongs

The unsounded /r/ has been included in the graphic representations. Some accents of English do pronounce the /r/, however.

Unvoiced consonants

Even with a greater number of consonant graphemes available to make the consonant sounds, one-to-one correspondence is low. Silent letters, doubling, and digraphs and trigraphs account for this.

Unvoiced and voiced pairs

Pairs are:
/s/ /z/
/ʃ/ /ʒ/
/f/ /v/
/θ/ /ð/

The first sound is unvoiced and the second voiced.

Literacy knowledge

Literacy

Literacy covers knowledge of grapho-phonics (see pages 97 and 98), spelling, punctuation, grammar, morphology, genre and structure, presentation, use of ICT, word-processing, CD-ROMs and the Internet. Other resources, such as non-fiction, film and media texts, are also important.

Useful texts

> Davison, J. and Dowson, J. (1998) *Learning to Teach English in the Secondary School.* Routledge. (chapters on reading, writing, grammar and computing.)
> DfEE (1998) *The National Literacy Strategy.* DfEE.
> Montgomery, D. (1997) *Spelling. Remedial Strategies.* Cassell.
> Moore, P. (1986) *Using Computers in English: A Practical Guide.* Methuen.
> Smedley, D. (1983) *Teaching the Basic Skills: Spelling, Punctuation and Grammar in Secondary English.* Methuen.
> Wray, D. and Medwell, J. (1997) *English for Primary Teachers. An Audit and Self-Study Guide,* (Section 3). Letts Educational.

Glossary

Term	Definition
accent	The way we pronounce words, according to our geographical and sometimes social position.
accented syllable	The stressed syllable(s) in a word.
active voice	A sentence in which the subject is the actor, as opposed to the passive where the subject is passive.
adjective	A word, such as *big, dead* or *financial*, that describes a person, place or thing; can be derived from verbs and nouns, using common suffixes such as *-ful, -ive* and *-y.*
adjunct	A constituent of the clause, that identifies where, when, how, or at what time something happened, e.g. *We are leaving in the morning.*
adverb	A word such as *quickly* or *now* that gives information about when, how, where, or in what circumstances something happens.
affix	A prefix or suffix, which may be derivational or inflectional, that is added to the beginning or end of a word.
agent	The object in a passive sentence: *The man was bitten by the dog.* May be omitted.
agreement	The matching of number of a noun or pronoun in the subject of a clause with the verb, i.e. subject-verb agreement.
allegory	A story with at least two meanings or possible readings, one on the surface and a second, deeper meaning.
alliteration	Close repetition of consonant sounds between words in poetry or prose.
allusion	An implicit or explicit reference to another text or work of art.
ambiguity	A word, such as a homonym, or text with uncertain or multiple meaning.
anapaest	A foot consisting of two unstressed syllables and one stressed syllable: *ĕbbĭng sēa.*
anaphora	Referring backwards, as in pronouns which refer back to previous nouns through anaphoric reference.
antithesis	Opposition of ideas, as in oxymoron.
antonym	Words that are opposites or used in opposition.
apostrophe	Two kinds are used in punctuation: apostrophes of possession and omission. There is also a literary usage.
archetype	A prototype or best example of an idea, object or character.
article	*A, an* and *the* – the indefinite and definite article.
assonance	Close repetition of vowel sounds in poetry or prose.
audience	The person or people to which a text is addressed or targeted, such as self, teacher, peer, examiner, unknown.
auxiliary verb	A verb such as *will, might, is, have, did* that comes before the main verb in a verb phrase, as in *He may have been* sitting in the lounge. Auxiliary verbs can be modal (giving information about likelihood and possibility – *may*) or temporal (giving information about tense – *have been*).
ballad	A poem in story form, usually with four-line stanzas in which two lines rhyme: abcb.
base	Used almost synonymously with root and stem, being the basis of a word before affixes are added. Common bases in English come from Greek or Latin.
bathos	A fall from the sublime to the absurd, as in anticlimax, for example.
bias	Sexual, racial or cultural bias, expressed by a writer or from a character's point of view.
bilingualism	The ability to use two languages.
blank verse	Unrhymed iambic pentameters, or lines of verse with five feet.
blend	A cluster of sounds that are blended together when spoken, as in *split.*
bound clause	Also called a subordinate clause – one that cannot stand alone as a sentence and must be joined to a free clause.
bound morpheme	A morpheme, such as *un-* or *-ness*, that cannot stand alone as a word and must be joined to a word or base.

Term	Definition
boundary marking	Punctuation marks that are used at grammatical boundaries: comma, semi-colon, full stop and capital letter.
burlesque	The best known example of this comic 'sending up' is Pyramus and Thisbe's play in *A Midsummer Night's Dream*.
caesura	A break in a line of poetry, often indicated by punctuation and by a metrical break.
case	The possessive (or genitive) case of nouns.
catharsis	A purging or release of emotion through experience as a reader or spectator.
cinquain	A five-line stanza or poem; the limerick is an example.
clause	A syntactic unit containing a verb. Clauses may be main or subordinate, finite or non-finite.
clause constituent	The syntactic units that make up the clause: subject, object, predicate, adjunct, complement.
cohesion	The process by which words in sentences, and sentences and paragraphs, are linked through reference substitution, lexical cohesion or ellipsis.
Common Underlying Proficiency (CUP)	The cognitive relationship between two languages, knowledge of which is used by people who are bilingual.
community language	The language common to a particular community whose use contributes to the community's identity.
complement	A constituent of the clause, coming after the verb *to be* (and similar link verbs such as *seems* or *appears*) and complementing the subject: *She was happy.*
complex sentence	A sentence consisting of two or more clauses in which one or more of the clauses is subordinate to the main clause.
compositional skills	The skills of spelling, punctuation, grammar, use of standard English and application of genre, used in writing.
compound sentence	A sentence consisting of two or more main clauses joined by co-ordinating conjunctions or punctuation.
compound word	A word formed by the joining of two words or bases, such as *blackbird*, but not an affix plus a base, such as *disappear*.
concrete poetry	Also called a 'shape poem', such as Herbert's altar poem, 'Easter Wings'.
conjunction	A word such as *and* or *because* that links together words or clauses: co-ordinating and subordinating conjunctions.
consonance	Close repetition of consonant sounds.
context	The internal context and external context of a piece of text relate to the surrounding words and to the audience respectively.
co-ordinating conjunction	A conjunction such as *and*, *but*, and *or* that joins words or main clauses.
couplet	Two successive rhyming lines.
dactyl	A foot consisting of one stressed and two unstressed syllables: *sāusăgĕs*.
declarative sentence	A sentence or clause that makes a statement.
deconstruction	The process of undoing or deconstructing a text to uncover meanings; a form of literary criticism.
derivation	The process of word formation by adding derivational prefixes and suffixes to words or bases to form other words.
determiner	A class of words, including articles, that are found before nouns: *the, some, its, those.*
dialect	A social or geographically located variety of language characterized by particular grammatical and lexical features: Cockney, Glaswegian, standard English.
digraph	Speech sounds that, when written, require two letters – vowel and consonant digraph: *moon* and *ship*.
diphthong	A long vowel sound in which two vowel sounds are very closely blended, as in *toy* and *ear*.
EAL/ESL	English as an additional language is a term that is preferable to English as a second language, because it considers English and any other language as complementary, rather than suggesting that English is a deficit language.
elegy	Elegy, Cuddon says, 'has come to mean a poem of mourning or lament'.
ellipsis	A feature of cohesion, which means that words or phrases can be omitted because they are understood from preceding text.
euphony	The pleasing sound produced in poetry and prose through phonological effects such as assonance and soft consonance.
eye rhyme	Rhyme which is apparent to the eye but which is not produced when spoken, as in *bushes* and *blushes*.
feminine rhyme	Rhyming of two syllables at the ends of lines, as in *bower* and *flower.*
feminist criticism	A critical process that examines and interprets literature from a feminist perspective, questioning masculine positions.

Term	Definition
field, tenor and mode	M. A. K. Halliday's terms, which he describes as 'the three features of the context of situation'. Field relates to what a text is, such as the field of law or medicine, and is similar to genre. Tenor relates to the participants and their status. Mode relates to the mode of the text: written or spoken, rhetorical.
figurative language	Figures such as metaphor, simile, personification, onomatopoeia, oxymoron.
finite clause	A clause containing a finite verb: *The dog has eaten the bone.*
finite verb	A verb that indicates tense and has a subject: *He was eating dinner*, but not *Being inquisitive*.
first language	For bilingual people, their first language can be the first language learnt, the home language, or the language used the most.
foot	A metrical unit, containing a particular combination of stressed and unstressed syllables: anapaest, iamb, trochee.
form	Forms of poetry, fiction and non-fiction are usually named: ballad, ode, dictionary entry, leader (newspaper), report, diary.
Formalism	The Russian formalists began this form of literary criticism, which links with structuralism.
free clause	A clause that is freestanding and can therefore be a sentence; sometimes called a main clause; contains a finite verb.
free verse	Non-rhyming verse, also with free metrical form.
generative grammar	A form of grammar originated by Noam Chomsky, whereby sentences are generated through a finite set of rules.
genre	Types of spoken or written texts that conform to a particular set of conventions and often have specialized vocabularies: narrative, procedural text (recipe), expository text (essay).
grammar	The study of syntax, phonology and morphology.
grammatology	A form of literary criticism that focuses on the written sign, although different from semiology. Derrida believed that signs are unstable and changing within a text. Grammatology is a way of using words in writing.
grapheme	The letters of the alphabet that are used to represent the sounds of speech, or phonemes.
grapho-phonic knowledge	Used in decoding text and in spelling, it relates to knowledge of the relationship between sounds and letters.
haiku	A Japanese poetic form consisting of 17 syllables in three lines of five, seven and five syllables respectively.
heritage language	The language regarded as the native, home, or ancestral language, which may be indigenous, such as Welsh or Gaelic.
heteronym	Words with the same spelling but different meaning, pronunciation and stress, e.g. *object, object*.
hexameter	A metrical line consisting of six feet.
home language	A general term referring to the most common language spoken in the home of bilinguals.
homograph	Words that are spelt the same but are not pronounced the same and have different meanings: *sow* meaning *scatter* and *pig*.
homonym	Words that are spelt and sound the same but have different meanings: *bear* meaning *carry* and the name of a type of animal.
homophone	Words that sound the same but are spelt differently: *air, heir, ere; mode, mowed; their, there, they're*.
hyperbole	A figure of speech; exaggeration for emphasis.
hyponym	A word included in a general set, e.g. *Alsation* and *Labrador* are hyponyms of *dog*.
iamb	A metrical foot, consisting of an unstressed and a stressed syllable: *begin*.
imperative sentence	A sentence or clause that makes an order: *Stop the train!*.
implied reader	In addition to and associated with the 'actual reader', the implied reader is the reader constructed by the text.
infinitive	Also called the 'to' form of the verb, it is the base form of the verb that you look up in the dictionary.
inflection	The process by which suffixes add grammatical meanings to nouns, verbs and adjectives: the plural marker -*s*, the possessive case, the past tense, participles, the third person, and comparative and superlative forms of adjectives.
internal rhyme	Rhyme within a single line of poetry.
interrogative sentence	A sentence that asks a question: *Are you coming for a drink?*
intransitive verb	A verb without an object: *He slept*.
irony	As in dramatic or romantic irony, involving paradox and discrepancies between expected events and reality; used in satire, comedy and tragedy.

Term	Definition
jingle	A poetic form that often uses alliteration and rhythm; many nursery songs and rhymes are jingles.
language diversity	A group's or individual's language repertoire, denoting a range of different languages, accents or forms.
language variety	The range of different forms of language: accent, dialect, register, standard and non-standard forms.
layout	Relating to the presentation of text to enhance meaning: use of paragraphs, fonts, bullets, sections.
lexeme	A linguistic term for 'word'.
lexis	A collective term for the words in a text, as opposed to the syntax or phonology.
limerick	A poetic form, being a cinquain of a particular type, with a generic system of meter and rhyme.
lyric poetry	The Romantic period is characterized by lyric poetry; it is usually thoughtful and expressive.
main clause	Also called a free clause, it is a clause that is capable of being freestanding as a sentence but which can also be combined with other free clauses to make a compound sentence, or with bound clauses a complex sentence.
masculine rhyme	A single-syllable rhyme as opposed to feminine rhyme.
metalanguage	The terms we use to talk about language, as in this glossary.
metaphor	Figurative language that involves referring to something through something else.
meter	The rhythm or metrical arrangement of feet: iambic pentameter, hexameter, trimeter.
Miscue Analysis	Used in the assessment of reading, paying special attention to the 'miscues' or deviations from the original text.
modernism	A movement in the arts, including painting, architecture and literature at the turn of the nineteenth century, which involved innovation.
monolingual	Proficiency in one language only.
morpheme	The smallest unit of meaning; words can consist of one or more morphemes; derivational and inflectional prefixes and suffixes are bound morphemes.
morphology	The study of the structure of words, their inflections and the process of compounding.
motif	Used synonymously with 'theme'; a repeated idea or object throughout a piece of literature (or music).
narrative	Involving a narrator, it can be written or spoken and covers a variety of forms: autobiography, diary, short story, novel.
neologism	A newly created or coined word in text.
non-finite clause	A clause containing a non-finite verb: *Sitting on the step, she thought about the day's events.*
non-finite verb	A verb without an indicator of tense and without a subject: *Being new to the job,* ....
non-standard English	English that uses non-standard grammar and lexis or meanings that are particular to it; a dialect.
nonce word	A new coinage or neologism.
noun	A class of words that refer to people, things or abstract ideas: *woman, table, compassion.*
number	A grammatical term used to describe whether a noun or verb is singular or plural; nouns and verbs must agree for number.
ode	A poetic form, which Cuddon describes as a rather grand 'lyric poem, usually of some length' with 'a marked formality of tone and style' and 'an elaborate stanza structure'.
object	A constituent of the clause that usually comes after the verb: *She ate a cake*; not present after intransitive verbs.
onomatopoeia	A figure of speech that describes words that imitate sounds.
organization	The organization of a text relates to its presentational, structural, grammatical and cohesive features.
oxymoron	A figure of speech that uses opposite words in close proximity for effect: *angry pleasure; pleased contempt.*
paradox	An opposition or apparent contradiction: *The careful keeping of a diary was careless.*
parallelism	Grammatical parallelism is a feature of rhetoric, well-written prose and poetry: *It was the best of times. It was the worst ....*
parody	Imitation of one text by another, in a mocking style, playing on the conventions of the original text; used in satire.
passive voice	An active sentence is transformed into the passive by reversing the subject and the object, so that the object becomes agent.
pathetic fallacy	An effect in literature by means of which nature is given human emotions.
pathos	The evocation of feelings of pity, sorrow and empathy; mournful mood.
pattern poetry	*See* 'concrete poetry'.

Term	Definition
personification	Where inanimate objects are given human qualities.
phoneme	The units of sound that make up speech.
phonological knowledge	Knowledge of the sound system, important to reading, spelling and the study of accents.
phonology	The study of the sound system.
phrase	A group of words that make up a clause constituent, such as the noun phrase forming subjects and objects in clauses: *the little red hen* saw *the sly old fox*.
plot	The design of a novel or play, made up of a particular sequence of events and features, such as opening, dénouement, resolution, ending, coda.
possessive	The possessive case is indicated by the use of an apostrophe: *dog's, dogs', Keats's, Jones's*.
predicate	A clause constituent consisting of a verb phrase, usually coming after the subject: *The group were singing a song*.
preferred language	A bilingual speaker's preferred language may differ, according to setting, purpose and audience.
prefix	A bound morpheme and derivational affix added to the beginnings of words: *interest, disinterest*.
preposition	A word class that includes words such as *in, on, towards, through*; gives information about position and location.
presentational skills	Skills that involve layout of text, handwriting, use of fonts, sections and arrangement of text, diagrams and pictures.
pronoun	A word class that includes words such as *I, he, we* and demonstratives: *those, these, this*.
psychoanalytical criticism	Literary criticism that uses psychoanalytical theory to interpret literature.
pun	Word-play involving words with dual meanings, used for humorous effect.
purpose	The purpose that a text is intended to serve affects its form, structure, tone and use of vocabulary.
reader-response theory	A theory originating from Wolfgang Iser, which describes the relationship between reader, writer and text.
Received Pronunciation	RP is the accent that is most associated with standard English, although standard English may be spoken with any accent.
register	The language used in a particular situation, formal or informal; use of particular intonation, as in the register of teachers.
root	*See* 'base'.
roundelay	Cuddon describes this as 'a short simple song ... where refrain and repetition are used extensively'.
satire	An attempt to ridicule or expose hypocrisy, as in Swift's *Gulliver's Travels* or Jane Austen's *Pride and Prejudice*.
scanning	A technique used in reading to find specific information, rather than reading for information.
schwa	The unstressed vowel sound produced in words like *independent* that makes spelling problematic.
semantic knowledge	Knowledge about meaning of a text can be gained through the text, its context, knowledge of the process of reading and world knowledge.
semiotics	A study of the signs used in literature, film and media, and how these contribute to meaning; see Umberto Eco (1981).
sentence	Simple, compound, complex and compound-complex sentences are classified in terms of the types of clauses they contain.
silent letter	Silent vowels and consonants found close to the beginning of words make them difficult to look up and spell: *psalm, guilt*.
simile	A figure of speech that makes a comparison between sometimes seemingly unconnected items: *Empty ships toss in the waves like surging emotions*.
simple sentence	A sentence containing a single main clause.
sociolinguistics	The study of language in society; accent, dialect, bilingualism and language diversity are within this area.
skimming	Skimming is a reading strategy that allows the reader to gain a general impression of what a text is about, whether the text is suitable for their immediate need and whether they want to read it.
sonnet	Petrarchan, Spenserian and Shakespearean are the three main types of sonnet based on the rhyme scheme over 14 lines.
spondee	A metrical foot consisting of two stressed syllables: *bēlls tōll*.
standard English	The dialect of English that has prestige status and is used in formal, national and international settings.
stanza	A verse or stanza is a collection of lines of poetry. A stanza may be short (2 lines) or long (14 lines).
status marking	The set of punctuation marks that indicate the status of a phrase or sentence: capitals, exclamation and question marks, brackets, pairs of dashes or single dashes, speech marks and single quotes.
stem	The base or root of a word as it is used with a suffix – the part that remains unchanged when the suffix is added.

Term	Definition
style	Involves grammatical, lexical, presentational, generic and idiosyncratic choices on the part of the author.
stylistics	The study of aspects of style using objective rather than subjective judgements of the contributions of grammar, lexis, rhetoric, semantics, meter and phonology to the meaning of the text.
structuralism	The study of texts, film and media using Saussurean linguistics.
subject	A clause constituent consisting of a noun phrase; in English the subject is often in sentence initial position: _It was a fine day. My father's closest friend_ was his old pal Richard.
subordinate clause	Also called a bound clause – one that cannot stand alone as a sentence and must be joined to a main clause.
subordinating conjunction	A conjunction, such as _because, if, while_, that introduces a subordinate clause and binds the clause to the main clause.
suffix	An affix, which may be inflectional or derivational, added to the end of words to make new words or create an inflection.

syllable	A unit consisting of a vowel sound and possible onset and final consonants:
	  elephant – three syllables: el-e-phant
	           VC-V-CVCC

syllabic segmentation	The process of dividing words up into syllables in order to read or spell them.
symbol	An object that stands for something else, such as the albatross in 'The Ancient Mariner' warning of danger.
synonym	Words that have the same or similar meanings, although there are no true synonyms as words are rarely interchangeable in all contexts and collocations: _circular – round._
syntactic knowledge	Knowledge about the structure of sentences and word order that makes comprehension of new words possible in reading.
syntactic unit	The grammatical units within sentences: word, phrase, clause constituent, clause.
syntax	The study of the grammar of the sentence, its arrangement of words, phrases and clauses.
systemic grammar	Also called systemic-functional grammar; a description of the grammar of language according to a system of inter-related networks, allowing for fine degrees of delicacy.
tanka	A Japanese poetic form, consisting of 31 syllables in five lines: five, seven, five, seven, seven.
tense	Strictly speaking there are only two tenses in English, past and present, as our verbs only inflect for these two; other temporal aspects are conveyed through the auxiliary verbs.
transitive verb	A verb with an object: _The dog ate its dinner._
trigraph	A sound of speech that, when written, requires three letters: _man_oeu_vre, ni_ght_.
trochee	A metrical foot consisting of a stressed and an unstressed syllable: _bounty._
verb	A class of words containing verbs such as _sing, apologize, appear, seem, do_ and the verb 'to be', also called the copula.
word class	Words are classified according to their functions: noun, verb, adjective.
word family	Collections of words derived from the same root or base: _magic, magician, magical; magnet, magnetism, magnetize, magnetic_; knowledge of word families helps with spelling, for example with the 'c' in _magician._

Further reading

Books mentioned in the text

Abbs, P. and Richardson, J. (1990) *The Forms of Narrative: A Practical Study Guide for English*. Cambridge University Press.

Aitchison, J. (1987) *Words in the Mind: An Introduction to the Mental Lexicon*. Blackwell.

Ayers, D. M. (1986) *English Words from Latin and Greek Elements* (second edition) University of Arizona Press.

Baker, C. (1994) *Foundations of Bilingualism and Bilingual Education*. Multilingual Matters.

Barthes, R. (1977) *Image-Music-Text*. Fontana (trs. S. Heath).

Berney, K. A. (ed.)(1994) *Contemporary British Dramatists*. St. James Press.

Blain, V., Clements, P. and Grundy, I. (eds.) (1990) *The Feminist Companion to Literature in English*. Batsford.

Burton, M. (ed.) (1989) *Enjoying Texts: Using Literary Theory in the Classroom*. Stanley Thornes.

Carter, R. (1987) *Vocabulary*. Allen & Unwin.

Carter, R. (ed.) (1982) *Language and Literature*. Allen & Unwin.

Carter, R. (ed.) (1990) *Knowledge about Language and the Curriculum: LINC Reader*. Hodder & Stoughton.

Chapman, J. (1983) *Reading Development and Cohesion*. Heinemann Educational.

Chevalier, Y. (ed.) (1993) *Contemporary World Writers*. St. James Press.

Collins COBUILD (1995) *Collins COBUILD English Dictionary*. HarperCollins.

Cope, B. and Kalantzis, M. (eds.) (1993) *The Powers of Literacy: A Genre Approach to Teaching Writing*. Falmer Press.

Coulthard, M. (ed.) (1994) *Advances in Written Text Analysis*. Routledge.

Crystal, D. (1987 and 1995) *The Cambridge Encyclopaedia of the English Language*. Cambridge University Press.

Crystal, D. (1996) *Rediscover Grammar* (second edition). Longman.

Cuddon, J. A. (1992) *The Penguin Dictionary of Literary Terms and Literary Theory* (third edition). Penguin.

Cummins, J. and Swain, M. (1986) *Bilingualism in Education*. Longman.

Davidson, C. and Wagner-Martin, L. (eds.) (1995) *The Oxford Companion to Women's Writing in the United States*. Oxford University Press.

Davison, J. and Dowson, J. (1998) *Learning to Teach English in the Secondary School*. Routledge.

Derrida, J. (1976) *Of Grammatology*. Johns Hopkins Press (trs. Gayatri Spivak).

DFE (1995) *English in the National Curriculum*. HMSO.

DfEE (1998)*The National Literacy Strategy*. DfEE.

DfEE (1998) *Teaching: High Status, High Standards*. DfEE (Circular 4/98).

Drabble, M. (ed.) (1985) *The Oxford Companion to Literature in English*. Oxford University Press.

Eco, U. (1981) *The Role of the Reader*. Hutchinson.

Fairclough, N. (1989) *Language and Power*. Longman.

Fletcher, P. and Garman, M. (1979) *Language Acquisition*. Cambridge University Press.

Foster, S. H. (1990) *The Communicative Competence of Young Children*. Longman.

Fowler, R. (1986) *Linguistic Criticism*. Oxford University Press.

Francis, G. (1994) 'Labelling Discourse' in: M. Coulthard (ed.) *Advances in Written Text Analysis*. Routledge.

Freeborn, D. (1986) *Varieties of English* (second edition). Macmillan.

Freeborn, D. (1996) *Style*. Macmillan.

Freeborn, D. (1998) *From Old English to Standard English*. Macmillan.

Gentry, G. R. (1981) 'Developmental Spelling' in *Reading Teacher*, Vol. 34, No. 4.

Graddol, D., Cheshire, J. and Swann, J. (1994) *Describing Language* (second edition). Open University Press.

Green, K. and LeBihan, J. (eds.) (1996) *Critical Theory and Practice: A Coursebook*. Routledge.

Greenbaum, S. (1990) *The Oxford English Grammar*. Oxford University Press.

Halliday, M. A. K. (1985) *An Introduction to Functional Grammar*. Arnold.

Halliday, M. A. K. (1989) *Spoken and Written Language*. Oxford University Press.

Halliday, M. A. K. and Hasan, R. (1976) *Cohesion in English*. Longman.

Hart, J. D. (1986) *The Concise Oxford Companion to American Literature*. Oxford University Press.

Hoey, M. P. (1991) *Patterns of Lexis in Text*. Oxford University Press.

Holmes, J. (1992) *An Introduction to Sociolinguistics*. Longman.

Hughes, A. and Trudgill, P. (1979) *English Accents and Dialects: An Introduction to Social and Regional Varieties of British English*. Arnold.

Kuiper, K. and Scott Allan, W. (1996) *An Introduction to English Language*. Macmillan.

Labov, W. (1972) 'The transformation of experience in narrative syntax' in W. Labov *Language in the Inner City*, pp. 354–396. Blackwell.

Lee, V. J. (ed.) (1987) *English Literature in Schools*. Open University Press.

Leech, G. (1969) *A Linguistic Guide to English Poetry*. Longman.

Leech, G. (1981) *Semantics* (second edition). Penguin.

Lewis, M. and Wray, D, (1996) *Developing Children's Non-Fiction Writing*. Scholastic.

Lewis, M. and Wray, D. (1997) *Extending Literacy: Children Reading and Writing Non-Fiction*. Routledge.

Lodge, D. (1988) *Modern Criticism and Theory: A Reader*. Longman.

Longacre, R. E. (1983) *The Grammar of Discourse*. Plenum Press.

MacDougall, C. 'The role of literature in a multicultural society' in: V. J. Lee (ed.) (1987) *English Literature in Schools*, pp. 102-108. Open University Press.

Malmkjaer, K. (ed.) (1991) *The Linguistics Encyclopedia*. Routledge.

Martin, J. (1989) *Factual Writing: Exploring and Challenging Social Reality*. Oxford University Press.

Montgomery, D. (1997) *Spelling: Remedial Strategies*. Cassell.

Montgomery, M. (1986) *An Introduction to Language and Society*. Methuen.

Moore, P. (1986) *Using Computers in English: A Practical Guide*. Methuen.

Ousby, I. (ed.) (1988) *The Cambridge Guide to Literature in English*. Cambridge University Press.

Oxford English Dictionary (1989). Clarendon Press.

Payne, J. (1995) *Collins COBUILD English Guides 8: Spelling*. HarperCollins.

Peccei, J. Stilwell (1995) *Child Language*. Routledge.

Peim, N. (1993) *Critical Theory and the English Teacher*. Routledge.

Pinker, S. (1994) *The Language Instinct*. Penguin.

Propp, V. (1958) *Morphology of the Folktale*. University of Texas Press.

Protherough, R. (1983) *Developing Response to Fiction*. Open University Press.

Protherough, R. (1995) 'What is a Reading Curriculum' in R. Protherough and P. King, *The Challenge of English in the National Curriculum*, pp. 30–47. Routledge.

QCA (1998) *The Grammar Papers. Perspectives on the Teaching of Grammar in the National Curriculum*. QCA.

Quirk, R., Greenbaum, S., Leech, G. N. and Svartvik, J. A. (1985) *A Comprehensive Grammar of the English Language*. Longman.

Robins, R. H. (1989) *General Linguistics: An Introductory Survey* (fourth edition). Longman.

Romaine, S. (1989) *Bilingualism*. Blackwell.

Sawyer, W., Watson, K and Adams, A. (eds.) (1989) *English Teaching from A-Z.* Open University Press.

SEAC (1992) *Pupils' Work Assessed – Key Stage 3: English.* SEAC.

Shattock, J. (1993) *The Oxford Guide to British Women Writers.* Oxford University Press.

Sinclair, J. (ed.) (1990) *Collins COBUILD English Grammar.* Collins ELT.

Smedley, D. (1983) *Teaching the Basic Skills: Spelling, Punctuation and Grammar in Secondary English.* Methuen.

Snowling, M. J. (ed.) (1993) *Children's Written Language Difficulties: Assessment and Management.* Routledge.

Thieme, J. (1996) *The Arnold Anthology of Post-Colonial Literatures in English.* Arnold.

Theory into Practice. Ohio State University.

Thomson, J. (1987) *Understanding Teenagers' Reading: Reading Processes and the Teaching of Literature.* Methuen Australia.

Torbe, M. (1978) *Teaching Spelling.* Ward Lock.

Trudgill, P. (1983) *Sociolinguistics: An Introduction to Language and Society* (revised edition). Penguin.

Wardhaugh, R. (1986) *An Introduction to Sociolinguistics.* Blackwell.

Wray, D. and Medwell, J. (1997) *English for Primary Teachers. An Audit and Self-Study Guide.* Letts Educational.

Wray, D. and Lewis, M. (1997) *Extending Literacy. Children Reading and Writing Non-Fiction.* Routledge.

Books from which extracts are used

Austen, J. (1965) *Persuasion.* Penguin (first published in 1818).

Austen, J. (1972) *Pride and Prejudice.* Penguin (first published 1813).

Carroll, L. (1994) *Through the Looking Glass.* Penguin (first published 1872).

Fowles, J. (1969) *The French Lieutenant's Woman.* Jonathan Cape.

Hughes, A. and Trudgill, P. (1979) *English Accents and Dialects: An Introduction to Social and Regional Varieties of British English.* Arnold.

Keats, J. (1988) *Selected Poems.* Penguin.

Pinker, S. (1994) *The Language Instinct.* Penguin.

Rhys, J. (1968) *Wide Sargasso Sea.* Penguin.

Shakespeare, W. *Julius Caesar,* Sanders, N. (ed.) (1967). Penguin.

Syal, M. (1997) *Anita and Me.* Flamingo.

Personal learning plan

The **personal learning plan** is a way of planning, recording and monitoring your progress. Use the photocopiable templates on page 111 as you work through the seven sections of the audit, identifying tasks that require further work. As you check your answers, refer carefully to the **feedback**, and make a note of your initial levels and areas of strength in the **initial record**. Note any weaknesses identified at this stage in the **action plan** and target ways of dealing with them, such as self-study, school-based observation and seminars provided through your course. You will find that much of your development results from planned course content or school-based tasks, so self-study will form only part of your progress. However, all of this can be recorded in your learning record, initially in the **action plan**, as you target needs, and later in the **update on progress** section, as these needs are met.

There may be areas where you need help. Check out what is available: tutors may offer tutorials or workshops; you can work with your fellow students in study groups; teachers and librarians may be able to help; a particular book may be beneficial; or particular seminars may cover the knowledge you require. Record all your progress in the **update on progress** section.

A subsequent **audit**, towards the end of your course, will allow you to check progress and target any remaining areas for development. For this purpose, reuse the audit and feedback in this book.

A section of your **personal learning plan** might look something like this:

Task: A

Initial Record	Action Plan
30 September Knowledge of terminology fairly secure. Happier with literary rather than linguistic terms. Scored 15 out of 20.	Use the glossary and other reference books to look up and check understanding of transitive and intransitive verbs, bound morpheme, ellipsis and homonym. Construct a personal glossary whilst reading, noting any new terms and meanings.
	Update on Progress **10 October** Now understand and can use terminology from audit. Other terms targeted are contained in my personal glossary at the back of this record. **21 November** Was able to use appropriate terminology in my written assignment about reading strategies.

The following table contains a checklist of sections and tasks to help you with creating your **personal learning plan** and monitoring its development.

Time will pass extremely quickly, so start as soon as you have carried out the audit and whilst checking your answers in the feedback.

Section	Task	Description	Initial Record	Action Plan	Update on Progress
Section A	Task A	Technical terms			
Section B	Task B1	Morphology and semantics			
	Task B2	Semantic relations			
	Task B3	Semantics and variation			
	Task B4	Phonemes and graphemes			
	Task B5	Phonemic and syllabic segmentation			
	Task B6	Phonology and poetic effect			
Section C	Task C1	Word class			
	Task C2	Word function			
	Task C3	Word order			
	Task C4	Cohesion within sentences			
	Task C5	Complex sentences			
	Task C6	Co-ordination and subordination			
	Task C7	Standard and non-standard grammar			
	Task C8	Grammar and punctuation			
Section D	Task D1	Textual cohesion			
	Task D2	Text structure, form and genre			
Section E	Task E1	Written versus spoken English			
	Task E2	Multilingualism and language variety			
	Task E3	Historical changes in English			
Section F	Task F1	Response to fiction and non-fiction			
	Task F2	Presentation of information and ideas			
	Task F3	Implication, undertone, bias, assertion and ambiguity			
	Task F4	Critical approaches			
Section G	Task G	Authors and texts			

Task:

Initial Record of Progress	Action Plan
	Update on Progress

Task:

Initial Record of Progress	Action Plan
	Update on Progress